W9-CEW-190

Color Rendering

Color Rendering

A GUIDE FOR INTERIOR DESIGNERS AND ARCHITECTS

• *Concept*   • *Exploration*   • *Process*

WEI DONG

McGraw-Hill

New York   San Francisco   Washington, D.C.   Auckland   Bogotá
Caracas   Lisbon   London   Madrid   Mexico City   Milan
Montreal   New Delhi   San Juan   Singapore
Sydney   Tokyo   Toronto

Library of Congress Cataloging-in-Publication Data

Dong, Wei.
    Color rendering : a guide for interior designers and architects /
Wei Dong.
        p.   cm.
    Includes bibliographical references and index.
    ISBN 0-07-018007-5 (hardcover)
    1. Interior decoration rendering.   2. Color in interior
decoration.   3. Architectural rendering.   4. Color in architecture.
I. Title.
NK2113.5.D66   1997
720'.28'4—dc21   96-47591
                                    CIP

McGraw-Hill

A Division of The McGraw·Hill Companies

Copyright © 1997 by The McGraw-Hill Companies, Inc. All rights reserved. Printed in the United States of America. Except as permitted under the United States Copyright Act of 1976, no part of this publication may be reproduced or distributed in any form or by any means, or stored in a data base or retrieval system, without the prior written permission of the publisher.

2 3 4 5 6 7 8 9 0   1IMP/1IMP   9 0 2 1 0 9 8 7

ISBN 0-07-018007-5

The sponsoring editor for this book was Wendy Lochner, the editing supervisor was Christina Palaia, and the production supervisor was Don Schmidt. It was set in Bembo by North Market Street Graphics.

Printed and bound by Print Vision.

McGraw-Hill books are available at special quantity discounts to use as premiums and sales promotions, or for use in corporate training programs. For more information, please write to the Director of Special Sales, McGraw-Hill, 11 West 19th Street, New York, NY 10011. Or contact your local bookstore.

Information contained in this work has been obtained by The McGraw-Hill Companies, Inc. ("McGraw-Hill") from sources believed to be reliable. However, neither McGraw-Hill nor its authors guarantee the accuracy or completeness of any information published herein and neither McGraw-Hill nor its authors shall be responsible for any errors, omissions, or damages arising out of use of this information. This work is published with the understanding that McGraw-Hill and its authors are supplying information but are not attempting to render engineering or other professional services. If such services are required, the assistance of an appropriate professional should be sought.

To my loving family

Contents

Foreword

Rendering is practiced for the purpose of not only illustrating design ideas, but for the evocation of the *qualities* of such ideas. Designers must, among their many other responsibilities, predict how a place will feel visually to its actual and proximate users. This is done by creating virtual spaces, forms, illumination, color, materials, texture, and pattern all on a two-dimensional surface— usually paper or a computer screen. The designer must create this virtual place using the hardware of the hand, eye, and media and the software of the mind. They must work efficiently and leave only the relevant visual clues.

Once rendering skills are acquired, they can be utilized for most other kinds of design illustration, from design drawing to quick conceptual sketching. These skills of course translate to the computer as well. One who acquires such skills by hand is also able to execute, evaluate, and revise computer illustrations much more easily and confidently.

This book is unique. Wei Dong offers the reader a "tool kit" of techniques which can lead to such skills. Designers who wish to create previews of their designs, vehicles by which they can convey their ideas of space and place to others, would be wise to accept this offer.

Michael E. Doyle
Author, *Color Drawing*

Acknowledgments

I would like to thank all my colleagues, publishers, friends, and students who gave me the encouragement and support to accomplish this project. In particular, I would like to express my appreciation to Professor Joy Blake who helped to draft and enrich the first two chapters. Thanks to Professor Joy Dohr and Kathleen Stumpf for reviewing the book. Also, I would like to thank Anna Stevens and Veronica Schroeder for their contribution to the first two chapters.

Introduction

During the last two decades, many changes have created special challenges in visual communication and the presentation of interior design. These changes include the availability of new construction materials, advances in presentation techniques, the changing nature of design practice, and a renewed emphasis on process in design education. The concept of integrating traditional measures, Computer-Aided Design (CAD), and other mediums in visualizing design has been adopted by both design education and professional practice. Thus, we need to better use and expand the strengths of each medium in order to better solve the complex problems faced by contemporary society.

Traditionally, manual color rendering covered various aspects of design with equal emphasis. We have depended on only one medium, a manual technique, using basic rendering tools such as markers, pencils, or pens, to visualize and communicate the design, as well as express our feeling of a particular space and our own personal style of rendering. We ask of this manual procedure that it do everything: transform a two-dimensional shape to a three-dimensional shape, generate a perspective, understand shade and shadow, do color studies, and show the effectiveness of specific materials. Because this is a tremendous task and we have a time limit, we usually only touch the surface of each aspect of what we attempt to communicate through manual drawings. Now we have the option of shifting some of those tasks from the traditional approach of color rendering to other mediums. For example, we can let the computer generate the perspective for us, and we can let the computer do the three-dimensional model. In this sense the electronic medium may more accurately and scientifically study color changes in shading and shadows.

Even though the electronic medium has very specific advantages, to study the manual rendering first is essential. It is only then that we can fully understand the options at our fingertips in communicating our design. For manual rendering, we should invest our time and energy in visualizing and then communicating the essence of the space and the objects within that space. We want to retain the sensitivity of the human touch in color manipulation and representation. Also, we need to study in depth the techniques, which enhance the nature of manual rendering and which no other medium can replace.

Interior design is no longer a luxury or just decorative. Now there is a need and a demand for the interdisciplinary approach where professionals work as a team to interpret an environment holistically rather than restricting themselves to their narrowly defined fields. The study of how we can better communicate our ideas and our sensitivity to interior environments is important to this holistic development. An understanding of the rendering of interior components and the illustration of surface materials and structures should share equal importance with the study of form and exterior structures of a building. This book will provide a thorough study of color rendering with concentration on interior components and the effectiveness of those components. The analytical explanations integrate the conceptual and creative processes, and the technical execution brings the color rendering to a new level of visual thinking, communication, and creativity.

The text provides definitions for the materials and the techniques necessary to refine the rendering, as well as quick sketches, which may be used as examples during the designers's creation. By using a practical instructional approach with both written and graphic steps, the text introduces the basic elements of rendering methods and techniques. Hints for success are included. The methods are easy to understand and to apply to interiors, while at the same time they are useful in a variety of design fields because of the general use of easily obtained markers, colored pencils, and paints.

The sequence of exercises helps build confidence in beginning students and provides reference material for professionals. A variety of renderings, which appear in various stages in the design process, not just the final presentation image, are carefully studied, making this book especially useful.

This book has two applications: as a study guide and as a reference. As a study guide, interior design, architectural students, and professional practitioners are able to sequentially study or refresh their color rendering abilities. Students and professionals may study from basic material to individual objects, eventually moving on to complex environments. Included in the appendix are additional line drawings to practice color rendering more efficiently by eliminating some of the steps in the construction of drawings. Studying the contents of the book and doing the exercises should build a solid foundation for visual communication and representation in interior architectural environments.

Another way to use this book is as a reference to satisfy an immediate need when already involved in a project. As an example, when a designer needs to render a lobby that has marble, wood, and glass in the design, he or she may choose only the area of the book that shows how to render these materials for practice, then apply the information in the rendered drawing.

Also, instructors of the previously mentioned students may use this book as a text for rendering courses as well as a general reference for studio courses.

Sometimes a long, involved text may limit readers' visual imagination and the chance to develop their own visual thinking and visual communication abilities. For the most part, this book tries to eliminate lengthy text explanation. Only the absolute necessities are highlighted. The explanations of renderings and the detailed information for each step have different emphases. For example, the explanation of how to render a chair may emphasize how to create strong three-dimensional legs to support the seat, while the emphasis of an explanation about rendering an armchair may be focused on how to create the fabric and how to use the white spot for the highlight. This book is not intended to be a prescription for rendering drawings but for using color rendering to study the visual creation, exploration, and communication processes. Throughout the book, the reader is encouraged to visually analyze the steps taken for completing each rendering and to study the difference between each step. Eventually, the reader will develop a personal visual communication and thinking style.

This book's intention is not to teach how to draw the exact color image that is illustrated in the pages but to encourage personal exploration of rendering style. Every individual design is different, just as drawing tools are different, such as different brands of markers or colored pencils. Readers bring different backgrounds to this book, so the text emphasizes procedure and thought processes for creating the image rather than dictating the outcomes. The color of your drawing does not necessarily have to look exactly like the one in the book. For example, while studying the rendering of a gray marble block, you may need to change the color palette to one that is specified in your design. The choice of a specific marker or brand of pencils is left up to the reader, leaving room for flexibility according to the reader's taste. The focus should be the rendering process and the procedure.

Showing you how to create a good rendering is not the only goal for this book. The hope is that the overall quality of your design will be improved. Your confidence in your visual communication and thinking ability should be enhanced. A good rendering should help you communicate better with your client, your instructor, or other designers. Most importantly, you should be able to visually refine your own design decisions and analyze your own design progress.

We face an overwhelming amount of new technology in every aspect of our lives, including design. What are the common backgrounds that technology shares with our traditional approach? What has changed in the design process and what has been relearned? Identifying what has been changed can reinforce the importance of what remains and require us to refine our knowledge of these techniques. Visual drawings have become an integral part of the design process that will no longer be seen as a special topic relevant only to experts. Color rendering is one of the major elements of the visual communication drawings.

Summary of Chapters

Chapter 1, Introduction to Basic Rendering Materials, identifies and defines the various materials used in color renderings. Chapter 2, Learning the Basics, focuses on the basic application of various mediums and their use in rendering simple objects. Chapter 3, Rendering Basic Building Materials and Their Finishes, demonstrates, in a sequential approach, how to render surfaces of materials used in established environments. It focuses on mixing the mediums to create the desired effects and on the ease and speed with which the materials can be developed. Chapter 4, Rendering Objects and Features in Interiors, provides sequential illustrations with explanations on how to render individual objects found in interiors. For each category, there is an explanation for one or more examples, showing how to render a typical object or groups of objects in that category. Similar objects are illustrated without a detailed explanation. And Chapter 5, Rendering Various Types of Interiors and Exteriors, takes the materials and finishes rendered in the previous chapter and applies them to various types of interior environments. Various ceiling treatments and light sources are introduced.

Chapter 1

Introduction to Basic Rendering Materials*

Understanding the capabilities of various materials used in color rendering can assist you in selecting appropriate tools and materials for effectively communicating the design. This chapter identifies and defines a variety of materials used in color renderings but functions only as an introduction, limited to the essentials needed to perform the exercises presented in the subsequent chapters of the book. There are many other drawing mediums and materials available on the market; this chapter only introduces the major supplies and mediums that have been used with the examples in the book. So, as you perfect your skills and experience, refer to more in-depth resources for a more complete discussion of color rendering.

_____

* Professor Joy Blake has helped to draft and enrich this chapter.

Drawing Surfaces: Paper

Paper structure

When viewed under a microscope, paper is seen as a complex web of interlocking fibers. The composition and treatment of the fibers, together with how the weave was formed, determine the characteristics of the paper. It is important to choose a paper compatible with a chosen medium.

Therefore, the composition of the fiber, the weight of the paper, and the tooth and finish are important characteristics to consider when choosing paper for your rendering.

Fiber composition

The fiber composition and construction determine the durability and permanence of paper. _Durability_ is defined as a paper's ability to retain its original qualities under use, including the ability to stand up to erasing and material application. The _permanence_ of paper is defined as the length of time the paper will maintain its integrity, including its resistance to disintegration over time and yellowing with age.

Weight

Paper is measured by two standards of weight. The United States' scale of measure is by pounds. If a paper is said to be a "90 lb paper," then 500 sheets with dimensions of 8½ × 11, or one _ream,_ will weigh 90 pounds. The other common scale is metric. Under this system, a paper with a listed weight of "250 gsm" weighs 250 grams per square meter. Most paper types are sold in a variety of weights.

Tooth

The _tooth_ of a paper refers to the small peaks and valleys of the fiber surface. The amount

1

of tooth determines the paper's ability to catch and hold some forms of pigment. A paper with tooth is required for applying certain mediums to a surface.

Surface finish

There are a number of common terms used to describe the surface finish of a paper. If a paper is described as having a *hot-press* (HP), *plate,* or *smooth finish,* then the paper is slick with almost no tooth. If a paper finish is *cold-press* (CP) or *vellum,* then the paper has a tooth, but it is often barely detectable; the surface texture feels like the texture of fine sandpaper. If a finish is described as *rough,* then it is an irregular, bumpy, or a laid surface. A *laid-surface* texture is the texture of the weave of the frame used to make the paper. It is a surface with closely spaced lines crossed perpendicularly by wider spaced lines. Other texture labels may be brand-specific and should be felt and closely examined to determine the finish and texture.

Types of paper

Broad categories of papers are defined by certain characteristics. The properties of several types of paper—tracing paper, print paper, and watercolor paper—should be considered when choosing your drawing surface.

Drawing papers are available for a variety of specific uses. *Bristol paper* is the strongest of all

drawing papers. It is also very durable and will stand up to much hard drawing and erasing. It is heavier in weight, comes in a variety of thicknesses, and is available with a plate or a vellum finish. The plate finish, due to the lack of tooth, is more appropriate for pen and ink or flat washes of color. The vellum finish will accept a variety of mediums: pencil, colored pencil, graphite sticks, medium to hard charcoal, hard pastel, oil pastel, pen and ink, airbrush, gouache, acrylic paint, and marker.

Charcoal and *pastel-specific papers* are interchangeable. They often come with an irregular or a laid finish. They will only stand up to light erasing before the surface is damaged. Charcoal and pastel papers are also available in a wide variety of colors.

Papers made specifically for drawing range from very inexpensive newsprint paper to expensive handmade paper. *Rag paper* is a commonly used type of drawing paper. One hundred percent rag paper (100 percent cotton fibers) is durable and has greater permanence than many other drawing papers since none of the fibers that are used break down over time. It is similar to bristol but is not as durable or as thick. Papers used specifically for drawing accept pencil, graphite sticks, colored pencils, charcoal, oil pastels, paint slicks, and very light pen and ink drawing. Markers can be used but will often bleed. Drawing paper is available in many different colors and sizes.

Transparent and *translucent papers* are papers constructed for use as overlays, rough sketches, and quick rendering. The paper is sold in a variety of weights, but all types are lightweight relative to most other papers. One type is tracing or sketch paper and is sold as rag or nonrag. It comes in white and canary, which is a yellow color, and is used most often at the beginning of the process. *Trace,* as it is commonly referred to, will accept pencil, colored pencil, pastels, crayon, light pen and ink, and most design markers. Another kind is *vellum* (a type of paper as well as a surface finish), used most often for final design drawings. It will accept pen and ink and any type of pencil lead. When a final drawing is completed on drafting vellum or mylar, a diazo print can be run. The transparency level of the vellum will affect the background tone of the final diazo print. Only fine quality drafting vellum, not trace vellum, is used for final design drawings.

Print paper, often referred to as *blueprint paper,* is the kind of paper a diazo print is run on to transfer the image from a mylar or vellum drawing. Print paper is most often white paper, but when an image is transferred, it will have lines the color of the specific paper used. Blue, black, and brown line paper are most common. The speed at which a print is run through the machine will determine the background of the paper. If a slow speed is chosen, the paper will remain relatively white. When the paper is run through moderately fast, the background will be toned the color of the lines. But when the paper is processed rapidly, it may make the lines difficult to distinguish. A toned background may be beneficial if the print is to be rendered. Print paper will not stand up to hard erasing but will accept pencil, marker, colored pencil, pastels, and pen and ink drawing.

Watercolor paper is specifically designed for watercolors but will accept other media depending on the specific surface finish. Watercolor paper is available with hot-press, cold-press, or rough finish. The cold-press finish is the most popular. The various finishes cause a variety of results with distinct reactions to the watercolor.

Rendering Mediums

Markers

The two most common marker systems used for rendering purposes are alcohol-based and xylene-based markers. The *base* is the vehicle that carries the pigment to the drawing surface. The alcohol-based markers are virtually odor free and are not hazardous to your health. The xylene markers have a very distinct chemical odor and require adequate ventilation for use since the fumes can cause respiratory and other health problems. The type of marker system you use depends on

your preference. The xylene pigments tend to last longer and not fade as quickly as the alcohol pigments. However, the alcohol-based markers are rapidly becoming the most preferred marker since they pose less of a health risk. Both types have their pros and cons depending on the user's experience and viewpoint. The examples in this book were rendered using alcohol-based markers. Both types of markers can be applied to numerous drawing surfaces. Neither type can be erased once it is applied.

Although not used as commonly, there are some good water-based markers on the market. Water-based markers provide great ease in blending and lightening tones by using a paintbrush or dampened cotton swab. Water-based markers are also very conducive to mixing mediums. Water-soluble markers have a flexible brush tip as well as a fine fiber tip, providing a variety of possible line qualities. Two water-soluble markers that are very useful for working in a more painterly style or for illustrations requiring soft forms as well as hard-edged images are the Staedtler Mars Graphic 3000 Duo, available in 100 colors, and the Tombow Dual, available in 72 colors, among which are 15 tones of gray.

Watercolor and gouache

There are two types of water-based paints that will be used in this book: watercolor and

gouache. They are typically applied with a paintbrush and mixed with water for a smoother application. Each can be applied in an opaque, thick manner or watered down to a transparent wash format. Each type of paint comes in a full range of premixed paint colors. Regardless of which colors you have, it is important to always have the basic black and white and the primary colors, yellow, blue, and red, on hand for mixing additional colors. These basic colors mixed in the correct proportions can produce numerous other custom colors without the cost of purchasing individual colors.

Care should be taken in selecting the proper working surface for using paints. The water in the paints will warp most boards or wrinkle the paper. It is best to use a board that has been designed for watercolor use. Typically, a medium-tooth board or watercolor board is the ideal working surface.

Watercolor is generally classified as a transparent color type. Watercolors should be used to cover large areas fast, and another medium should be used for doing details. Watercolors traditionally do not work well for doing the detailed part of a drawing. They work best when used in conjunction with other mediums, such as colored pencils.

Gouache (opaque paint) is ideal to use when opaque surfaces or materials are being rendered. Goauche is available as a tube paint or in dry pots, which come in a wide variety of colors. Gouache is considered an opaque medium when used directly out of the tube. It can also become very transparent by diluting it with water. Gouache is not erasable but can easily be painted over, reworked, or lifted off the board by using a brush filled with water.

Colored pencils

Colored pencils come in a wax base, water-soluble, or pastel-based format. Wax-based pencils are the most common. The wax-based pencil blends easier and covers larger areas faster than the other types; they also break easier and require constant resharpening. Pastel-based pencils are the smoothest and most blendable pencils available. Water-soluble-based pencils capture the best of both by providing blending and detail qualities all in one. The water-soluble base is soft but not brittle.

Colored pencils offer a wide variety of intense colors. Pencils can be purchased individually or in variously sized sets. This medium is excellent for drawing details. Colors can be easily blended by using a blending pencil, marker blender, or with rubber-cement thinner applied to a cotton tip. Water-soluble colored pencils can also be blended with a damp brush or cotton tip. Color pencil marks can sometimes be erased by using a plastic or pink eraser.

Lead pencils

Like other drawing tools, personal preference also plays a role in which pencils you use for drawing and rendering purposes. There are basically three pencil designs: wood, lead holders, and mechanical pencils. The *wood pencil* is the typical hexagon-shaped pencil with lead encased in wood. *Lead holders* and *mechanical pencils* are hollow metal or plastic pencils into which lead is loaded. The lead holder holds a thicker diameter piece of lead than the mechanical pencil. Sharpening the lead in the holder requires a special sharpener called a *lead pointer*. The lead of the mechanical pencil never needs to be sharpened because of its tiny lead size, which produces a tiny point. Both the lead holder and mechanical pencil have a release button in the top to allow the lead to be pushed down into the tip.

Various types of lead can be loaded into the lead holder and mechanical pencil. There are 18 different types of lead used in pencils. The lead types vary in degree of hardness, which is denoted by a letter and/or number located on the pencil end or on the lead package. The softer leads are primarily used for rendering purposes and the harder ones for drafting. Lead comes in the following types: 6B to B, HB, F, and H to 8H. The softer leads are 6B through HB, and the rest are classified as hard leads.

Softer leads wear down quicker and require more sharpening. They also make darker and thicker marks than the hard leads. Hard leads make very light and thin marks. Care should be used when drawing with hard leads. Too much hand pressure on the lead while drawing will cause the lead to rip the drawing paper.

TIP Use an HB lead to do the preliminary outline of a drawing before it is rendered. A 2H or 4H lead works well for creating lighter values for pencil renderings.

Equipment to Assist the Drawing and Rendering Process

The equipment necessary to assist in the drawing and rendering process can vary depending on individual style, preference, and expertise. To draw without any assistance from drawing equipment is referred to as a *freehand drawing technique*. To achieve a well-developed freehand style takes a lot of practice and skill. Therefore, it is recommended, especially for beginners, to use drawing equipment because mark making is easier, cleaner, faster.

Basic drawing and rendering equipment may include: a drawing board to support the paper, straight edges, erasers, and tape for securing the rendering paper or board to the table or for masking out areas on the drawing. Other tools that can assist in mark making and rendering are: straight edges, erasers, drafting tape, French curves, flex curves, and templates (circles and ovals). Some objects and materials found in your home can also assist in the rendering process. These may include: toothbrushes for splattering paint; cooking pot rims as templates for drawing large circular shapes; sandpaper or textured fabrics placed under the drawing paper for creating patterns while marking on the paper; and unusual paint applicators such as sponges, cotton-tipped swabs, and swatches of fabric for different textures and stroke marks.

 Experiment with different household objects and materials for assisting in the mark making process. Your motto should be, "Anything goes. If it works, then use it!" Be creative!!

It is important that all drawing and rendering equipment be kept clean and in good working order. Be careful that the rendering medium does not damage the equipment.

TIP To help protect the plastic edges of drawing equipment, cover them with a long, single piece of drafting tape. When the tape becomes dirty, replace it with a clean piece.

TIP Keep paper towels handy for fast and easy cleaning of drawing equipment during mark making.

The following sections provide a brief overview of some basic equipment used to study color rendering with this book.

Straight edges

Straight edges are considered one of the most important pieces of equipment needed for doing any type of rendering. Most mark making with markers and pencils requires the assistance of a straight edge. The most common ones used in rendering include: both regular and adjustable triangles, parallel bars, T-squares, drafting machines, mat board strips, rolling rulers, edge marker guides, and regular rulers.

Which ones or how many straight edges are needed depends upon user preference. One tool may work for one type of rendering and not for another. Experiment for the best results.

Triangles

Triangles are used for making vertical or diagonal marks. Triangles work best when used in conjunction with either a parallel bar or T-square. The parallel bar or T-square keeps the triangle from sliding up and down on the drawing table, thus keeping the trian-

gle in the correct position while making marks. The triangle needs to rest on the parallel bar while making vertical marks.

There are numerous sizes of triangles, from very large to very small. There are also two types of triangle styles: regular and adjustable. Both styles come with either a regular straight or a beveled (inking) edge. The regular triangle has three fixed edges and angles. The adjustable one can be changed to a variety of angles, providing a variety of different line and angle possibilities. A handy feature on the adjustable triangle is the angle adjustment knob projecting from its surface. This knob works well for holding, sliding, and quickly removing the triangle during use.

TIP You can buy a plastic self-sticking knob that can be attached to triangles. Check with your drafting or art supply store.

For rendering purposes, it is better to have a beveled, raised, or inking edge on all triangles. This type of edge is raised up off the drawing surface, which stops the wet medium being applied from smearing or bleeding under the edge of the triangle.

TIP Take coins (pennies or dimes) and tape them onto the flat surface away from the edges of a noninking or beveled-edge triangle. The coins will raise the

triangle up enough so that the edge of the triangle will not come in contact with the marks being applied to the drawing surface. This new raised triangle can now be used just like any inking triangle. Be careful not to secure the coins too close to the edge of the triangle because it will cause a bump in the line while drawing.

Parallel bars, T-squares, and drafting machines
Parallel bars and T-squares are used for drawing horizontal lines and to hold the triangle and other drafting equipment from sliding down the drawing board. A drafting machine is also used for drawing horizontal and diagonal lines. Drafting machines are designed to be angled in many directions, giving numerous line possibilities; however, they do not seem to be very common or popular for assisting in the rendering process.

Both parallel bars and drafting machines must be permanently attached to a drawing board or table. This is not true for T-squares. A T-square requires a board edge to keep the *T* part of the square plumb. A T-square requires a lot more skill to manipulate than a parallel bar or drafting machine. Most people prefer a parallel bar over the other two choices.

All three of these—whether metal, plastic, or hardwood—come in various lengths and with inking or regular edges. The metal ones

are easier to clean and last forever. However, a clear plastic edge gives the user the ability to see under the edge, which is useful in pinpointing exact locations.

Regular ruler
A regular ruler has two edges for assisting with line making. A big advantage of using a ruler is that it comes in almost any length, which is useful when long lines are needed. Rulers may be plastic, wood, or metal. Most metal rulers come with a cork backing. The cork raises up the metal edges to prevent smearing and to prevent the ruler from sliding off or around the drawing surface.

Mat board strip
A very popular and very effective straight edge that works well with markers is a mat board strip. The length and width of the strip can be cut to whatever size you need. The strip absorbs the marker against the edge, preventing any bleeding or smearing of the marks on the rendering surface. Another nice feature about using a strip is that when the sides of the strip get saturated with marker color, it can be recut or discarded for another piece.

 Try cutting different nicks and notches in the edge of the mat board strip for some interesting line styles and textures.

Edge-marker guide
The edge-marker guide is mainly used with marker applications. The guide is a strip of plastic that has two different raised-up or angled edges. The raised edges prevent the tip of the marker from touching the edge of the guide. This feature stops the markers from smearing with the guide. The design of the guide makes it easy for the user to hold and move it during mark making. The guide comes in different lengths to accommodate different widths of papers and boards.

Erasers and eraser shields

There are all types and shapes of erasers available. It is very important to always keep the eraser clean to prevent unnecessary smears.

One of the best tools for erasing is an electric eraser. An electric eraser is a timesaving tool when large areas need to be erased quickly and completely. When loaded with the correct type of eraser, it will remove all evidence of pencil marks and lighten or remove pen and marker marks from the paper. The electric eraser uses special sizes and types of erasers. Electric erasers are either rechargeable battery-operated types or electric types. A nice feature that prevents erasing holes in the drawing paper is an auto-stop feature that turns the machine off if too much pressure is exerted on the paper while erasing.

To assist in the erasing process, use an *eraser shield*. This flat metal piece is shaped like a credit card and has various shapes cut out of its surface. These shapes serve as a template for erasing. The metal surface prevents the shield from being destroyed during erasing. This shield is a quick way to erase out shapes on the drawing. The edge of the shield also can be used to clean up edges of lines.

Brushes

Variables that effect the handling and qualities of brushes are the handle length, ferrule shape, brush shape, and brush material.

The handle lengths are generally viewed as short or long. Long-handled brushes are best used for painting on an easel. The majority of illustrators, however, work close to the drawing surface, making short-handled brushes more comfortable to use.

The *ferrule* is the metal ring or cap that shapes the base of the brush and attaches the bristles to the handle. Flat and round ferrules are the shapes used for illustrations in this book and those most often used for interiors and architectural illustration.

Brush shape is produced by the shape of the ferrule and the shaping of the tip. Round brushes should produce a fine point and a flat brush will have a squared-off edge, producing right angles and hard edges.

Watercolor requires a soft rather than a stiff brush. Materials used for the hairs of a brush usually indicate its quality. The question of natural versus synthetic hair is one of both quality and cost. Natural hair is more costly and can be of higher quality; however, contemporary nylon brushes of high quality can often compete with natural hair and cost less.

Desirable traits to look for in a brush are the ability to hold a high volume of paint and to maintain its shape. The more hair a brush has, the more paint it is capable of holding, making work time more efficient. To find a brush with a good point, work it gently in water for a short time to remove the sizing. Make several strokes on paper, rewet the brush, and shake it hard. The shape should return to a fine tip. Keeping a brush clean and carefully stored will improve its life expectancy. When a flat brush is new, it should have square edges when viewed from the front (the wide side of the brush). From the side, the bristles should meet in a fine upside-down v shape. With lengthy wear, a flat brush will start to lose its square edges and may separate at the tip when viewed from the side. Wetting such a brush should revive the tip.

Illustrations in this book were all produced using three brushes: a 1¼ in flat, a ⅝ in flat, and a size 7 round, all having short handles and natural hair bristles. Wider flats are excellent for achieving large wash or color areas; you can work quickly and blend or grade colors or washes easily. A ½- or ⅜-in flat is the workhorse for this kind of illustration. It is used for basic forms and large detail areas. Because the majority of visual information is provided with this brush you may find it helpful to have two: one for dark and one for light colors, or one for color and one for blending with clear water. Round watercolor brushes range in size from 00, the smallest and sometimes referred to as a 5-hair brush, to size 20. A size 7 is a good medium size to work with for fine detail work and highlighted or shadowed edges. You can make very different mark qualities with a size 7 depending on the amount of pressure you use. Light pressure can produce a fine line like you would get with a very small brush, yet it can hold a much larger volume of paint. This allows you to work quickly and accurately at the same time.

Chapter 2

*Learning the Basics**

A solid foundation in rendering skills is the key to success in visually communicating your design. This chapter introduces the basic rendering techniques, which will be used in later chapters. By following the explanations for the techniques presented in the illustrations, you can acquire confidence applying the basic drawing techniques using a variety of mediums.

Mixing Colors

For each rendering medium there is a different method of mixing colors and a number of variables that will affect the finished quality of your work. Experimenting and making

---

* Professor Joy Blake has helped to draft and enrich this chapter.

samples are the best ways to arrive at the look you are after.

Markers

There are three ways to mix with a marker:

1. Layering two or more colors over one another, mixing the color on the paper
2. Applying two or more colors side by side, achieving the illusion of color mixing (as in pointillism)
3. Tip-to-tip mixing where you hold two markers together, allowing the colors to mix on the tips of the markers themselves

The paper and the base carrier of your marker (water, xylene, alcohol) are the variables that affect your work. The pressure

which you apply, the speed with which you work, and the number of layers you put down will all affect your value results.

Paper qualities to consider are absorbency, opacity, and tooth or texture of the surface. Since there are numerous varieties of papers on the market, we will limit our discussion to the general characteristics of paper rather than brand names. As a rule, when using markers, a less-textured paper is desirable. The more the tooth, the rougher and less even your final solution will be. Transparent tracing papers or vellum can be worked from both sides of the paper, providing a variety of textural qualities. The surfaces of a vast majority of transparent papers are smooth and nonabsorbent. Nonabsorbent papers may also be called bleed-proof or nonpenetrating. Opaque papers come in a range of absorbencies.

If you are using a water-soluble marker, the mixing process is much like that for watercolor paint. Results with xylene and alcohol-based markers are very similar. The examples shown in this book were rendered with alcohol-based markers.

Absorbent papers, more so than a nonabsorbent, will produce a rich, deep color quality, suggesting the illusion of greater depth. Absorbent papers will bleed, carrying the color beyond the point at which the marker makes contact with the paper. This produces a soft edge that can be very desirable when blending colors together. Color mixing is most successful working from light to dark when using an absorbent paper.

Figure 2-1 shows the use of markers on absorbent paper.

Bleed-proof paper may have a slight absorbency, retaining the best qualities from both paper extremes. Working from dark colors to light colors on opaque bleed-proof paper produces the most successful mixing. Figure 2-2 demonstrates markers on bleed-proof paper.

Transparent tracing papers, vellum, and illustration films do not absorb marker. The color sits on top of the paper, requiring a longer drying time and allowing for wet blending or mixing of colors. Figure 2-3 shows the use of markers on 100 percent cotton drafting paper. Figure 2-3a shows color layering, working from light to dark. Notice that the colors do not mix well using this approach. Figure 2-3b shows color layering, working from dark to light while the markers are wet. Notice the blue mixes with the red, darkening it, and the red and blue mix with the yellow, turning it muddy. While this can sometimes be a desirable effect, it is important to understand that on a nonabsorbent surface, any wet layering will result in blending, producing a color mix. If you work this way, your marker colors will become contaminated unless you develop a habit of cleaning them by rubbing the tips on a piece of scrap paper until they mark the true color

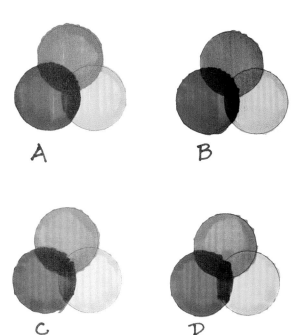

Figure 2-1 *Markers mixing on absorbent paper: (a) light to dark color on xerox paper (recycled product); (b) dark to light color on xerox paper; (c) light to dark color on 65-lb sketch paper (recycled product); and (d) from dark to light on 65-lb sketch paper.*

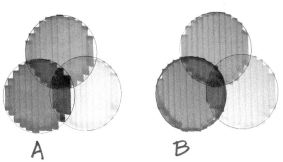

Figure 2-2 *Markers mixing on bleed-proof paper: (a) dark to light color on a smooth surface, bristol paper, 100 lbs; (b) dark to light color on bleed-proof paper for pens, 74 lbs.*

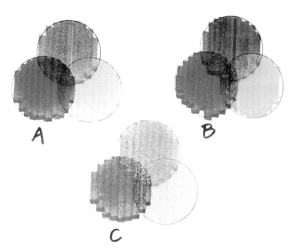

Figure 2-3 *Markers mixing on 100 percent cotton drafting paper: (a) color layering, working from light to dark; (b) color layering, working from dark to light while markers are wet; and (c) color mixing by layering dark to light while allowing one color to dry completely before applying the next.*

again. Figure 2-3c shows color mixing by layering dark to light while allowing one color to dry completely before applying the next. Note that the yellow still picks up some of both the blue and red, muddying it.

By placing two or more colors side by side on your paper, your eye will mix colors together, giving the illusion of physical color mixing. This technique is less successful with marker than with colored pencil, but it can provide wonderful textural qualities in some applications.

Tip-to-tip mixing is achieved by holding two different colors of marker together, allowing them to mix on the tips of the markers. Notice when two colors similar in value are mixed, as with the red and blue, the color mixed on each pen tip is different but equally successful. However, when a lighter value is mixed with a darker value, as with the yellow and blue or the yellow and red, the lighter-value marker carries the mix much more successfully than the darker-valued marker. Figure 2-4 illustrates this mixing technique. When using this technique you must clean your markers as previously discussed.

Water-based paints: watercolor and gouache

There are three ways to mix with watercolors:

1. Mixing color on a palette or in a container by adding two or more colors
2. Wet blending or mixing color on your paper surface
3. Laying glazes over one another by allowing one layer to dry before applying the next

Variables affecting color mixing with watercolor may include: the choice of paint, gouache, or transparent watercolor; and the tooth and quality of the paper. The amount of water you use will affect the value and transparency more than the color but should be taken into consideration while premixing color.

Assuming that a medium- to small-toothed illustration board or watercolor

Figure 2-4 *Tip-to-tip mixing technique for markers.*

paper is used, mixing color with gouache or transparent watercolor works much the same. Consistency of the paint must be between the consistencies of milk and paste. You can use a small container or a palette to mix on. Mixing palettes can be purchased in a variety of styles, but all you really need is a clear or white surface, such as a dinner plate or a piece of glass with the edges taped to protect from cuts. Mixing surfaces that are colored or have colored areas on them will distort the color you mix and it will appear different on your white paper.

It is generally faster to arrive at your desired color if you start with the lightest value of the two or more colors you are mixing, and add the darker value(s) to it. Knowing your color wheel or having a copy of it in view will make your early color-mixing experiences easier and faster.

Once you have mixed your color, you can apply it to a dry or wet surface. If you are working on a wet surface, the paper or board should have an evenly shiny glaze to it. Puddles or dry areas on the paper will not accept the paint evenly. The amount of tooth and water on the surface will affect the value and texture of your final solution rather than the color.

Wet blending or mixing color on your paper surface requires quick work. You must introduce your second color before your first has had the opportunity to dry. You can actually mix a number of colors by going back to your color palette repeatedly and introducing new colors to the damp colors on your paper. Using this method you can do the color-wash progressions commonly required for sky treatments or large wall areas. Again, working from light to dark usually produces the best results.

Glazing layer over layer of color produces a greater depth to the finished look than mixing on the palette. It is an approach that is more suitable for smaller areas or details rather than large areas of your work. If you choose the same colors as you did when mixing or wet blending the colors, your results will not appear the same when using a dry-glaze mixing method.

Colored pencils

The three ways of mixing with colored pencils are:

1. Layering two or more colors over one another
2. Applying two or more colors side by side, allowing the eye to mix the color
3. Using a combination of these techniques with a water-soluble color pencil

Variables affecting work in colored pencil may include: the base or carrier of the color (wax base, water-soluble, or oil base), the

tooth or texture of the paper, the pressure you apply, and the surface you are working on.

The key variable to color mixing when using colored pencil is the base and hardness of the pencil. Paper will affect the texture and depth. The working surface and amount of pressure you apply will affect the value and coverage. When using the same pencil, you will get a more even coverage and a darker appearance if your working surface is padded by several layers of paper than if you are working on a hard surface.

The quality and feel of the pencil contribute to the color. You may find some color ranges are more to your liking in one brand than another (see Figure 2-5).

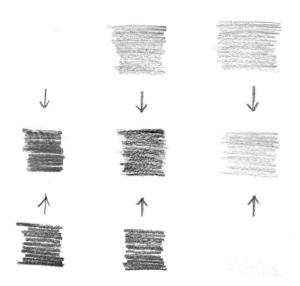

Figure 2-5   *Colored pencils mixing.*

When layering two colors over one another, it may be necessary to repeat one of the colors to get the desired mix. Both methods of working dark to light or light to dark will be effective with colored pencils. Layering complementary colors will mute the color on your paper. Depending on the balance of each complement, it may produce a neutral brown or gray color. Also, white does not layer well on some colors. It is best to test and experiment before applying to the final drawing.

Basic Application of the Mediums

Before the rendering medium can be applied, the drawing needs to be lightly sketched with a pencil on the final drawing paper or board. The amount of detail drawn in at this time depends on individual preference. If you are skilled with perspective drawing and feel comfortable in creating detail as you render, then only sketch the basic shapes and form on the drawing. If this is not for you, then draw in everything before color application begins. Usually the basic outline with some detail is sufficient to begin the rendering process.

 Draw a small sketch of what the drawing will look like on a separate piece of paper before starting the drawing.

TIP Try using a red or blue pencil instead of a graphite pencil for drawing. These colors will blend into the final drawing, creating color interest.

A technique that is used to transfer drawings on paper to a nontransparent paper or board (like watercolor paper or bristol board) uses graphite paper. The graphite paper is like carbon paper, but the marks are erasable, unlike the ink from the carbon paper. To transfer the drawing from paper onto the rendering paper or board, put the graphite paper on top of the board. Then put the original drawing on top of the graphite paper. Once stacked correctly, trace the drawing, and the graphite paper will transfer the drawing to the board.

Another technique is to sketch the image on a drawing paper, then use a copy machine to copy onto an appropriate rendering paper or board. (Some copy machines will accept thick boards.) Most of the time a messy-looking drawing looks cleaner when a copy is used for rendering purposes. Also, some of the smears or blobs created by the copy machine can be useful in creating textures and values in the final rendering.

TIP Make multiple copies of an original drawing to practice rendering techniques or to try out various color schemes and designs before the final one is started. This tip also helps keep the original safe in case of an accident, or if the rendering techniques do not work, you will always have a spare for trying again.

TIP Practice with your markers to see if they work well with a copy print. Some markers will make the black lines on a copy bleed, resulting in the colors going dirty. Usually alcohol-based markers are better for rendering copies than xylene-based markers.

Drawing techniques

Mark making with specific mediums

Markers. Markers basically come with five types of points: sharp, round, blunt, pointed, and brush tip. There are two styles of markers sold today: a single tip or double-ended tip. The double-ended type provides you with two different mark-making possibilities: thin and thick marks.

Alcohol-based markers come with a double- or single-ended tip system. Xylene-based markers come only with a single-ended tip.

The wide-tip markers are typically used for covering large areas very quickly and easily and for shading or shadowing in the bottom part of an object. The thin tip is used mainly for drawing in details on a drawing, for cleaning up edges of the drawing, and for drawing in the structure or outline of the object. Figure 2-6 demonstrates these uses.

Markers are typically held the same way as you would hold a pencil when writing. However, this may vary depending on certain techniques being executed. These techniques will be described in detail throughout the text.

Marking with a straight edge is the preferred application method for applying values or color to inanimate objects. A freehand application technique is typically used for creating value and color on living objects and for objects that require a more free-flowing profile, such as puffy sofa cushions or plants. This freehand technique can also be used for blending marker colors. Regardless of the applica-

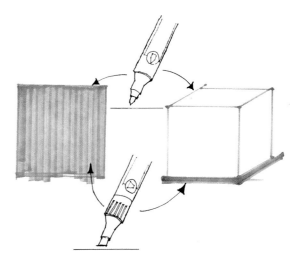

Figure 2-6   *The usage of the broad edge and the fine tip of the marker.*

tion method, it is important for the beginner to execute marks with skill and accuracy, using the appropriate marker technique.

TIP Try different types of straight edges to see which one works best for you. Try a regular or adjustable triangle with a parallel bar, or a piece of mat board cut into a strip, and/or a rolling ruler. Regardless of what works best, make sure the edge is beveled or raised up and that the edge is kept clean to prevent smearing of the marks.

Watercolor paints.   To paint with brushes requires holding the brush in a similar position as a pencil when writing. To steady the brush while doing details or while painting straight lines, hold the brush and extend the pinky finger onto the paper surface while making the marks. The extended finger serves as a crutch to steady your hand.

TIP A technique to help make straighter lines while using a paint brush is to run your pinky finger against a straight edge while making marks. The straight edge will serve as a line guide for your hand.
A more exact way to make a straight line while painting is to mask out the area that is above and below the line with tape, leaving a gap for painting the line. When the mask is removed, a painted line remains.

To create a more transparent painted surface, keep the paintbrush tip full of water and color during application. For a more opaque look, keep the brush tip dry of water and full of the liquid color. Try varying the amount of water and liquid color on the brush tip for numerous application techniques.

TIP Keep a paper towel handy for cleaning the excess water out of the paintbrush tip.

Pencils.   To make marks with pencils, there are generally two ways to hold the pencil: (1) straight up, and (2) at an angle. The pressure applied also is important in affecting the amount of color laid down. See Figure 2-7.
The straight-up technique requires holding the pencil just as you do when you are writ-

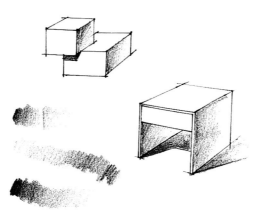

Figure 2-7   *Pencil gradation.*

ing. This straight-up technique is used for drawing lines and details in renderings.
The angle method requires holding the pencil with the index finger and thumb, resulting in the marks being made with the side of the pencil tip. This technique is used for shading, shadowing, and texturing renderings. This is useful for doing gradations of values especially on curved surfaces.
The point of the pencil can be either sharp or dull when making marks. The sharp tip is used for making crisp lines for outlining objects and details. The dull tip is used for fuzzy or soft lines that shade objects and create textures in renderings.

TIP Hold the pencil 2 or 3 inches back rather than at the point to help achieve a more expressive line quality and a relaxed hand.

Line techniques
All renderings are composed of numerous lines. Line styles and techniques will vary with the object being rendered. Most line work is created with a straight edge or by freehand. Regardless of the type of line, great care and skill in its execution is required.

Straight lines.   There are basically four ways to create straight lines when rendering:

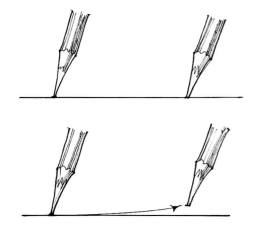

Figure 2-8 *Demonstration of the slow-line* (top) *and the lift-stroke line* (bottom) *techniques.*

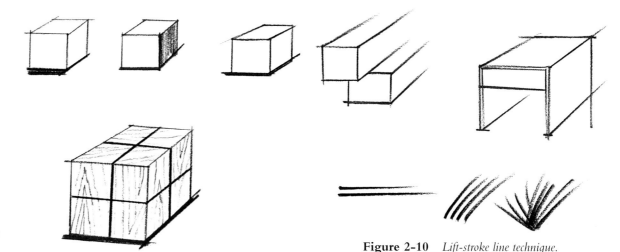

Figure 2-9 *Slow-line technique.*

Figure 2-10 *Lift-stroke line technique.*

1. Slow lines
2. Lift-stroke lines
3. Dry lines
4. Quick stroke

1. *Slow lines.* This technique requires a slow and precise application of marks on the paper, using an even hand pressure on the marker or pencil against the straight edge. The line is solid from end to end. This technique is useful for making shadows with the wide tip of the marker and for outlining with the thin tip of the marker. See Figure 2-8 (*top*) and, 2-9 for an illustration of this technique.

2. *Lift-stroke.* The application of this technique is quick and not as precise as the slow-line technique. This technique requires drawing a line by pushing hard, then, gradually lifting the marker or pencil up as the line ends (see Figure 2-8 (*bottom*) and 2-10). The end result is a line that starts out dark then gradually ends light. To keep the lines from looking messy, always use a straight edge during this mark-making process.

3. *Dry line.* Using the slow- or quick-stroke techniques, substitute the marker for a dried-up or old marker or a very dull pencil point. The final results will be marks that are not solid and appear textured (see Figure 2-11). The use of this technique is wide and varied, from textured fabric to the faces of rough brick—the possibilities are endless.

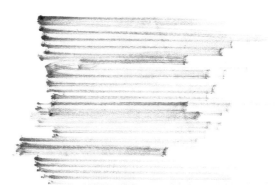

Figure 2-11 *Dry lines.*

4. *Quick stroke.* Using a straight edge, make quick and even lines. This technique is useful when filling in solid areas and for applying light values to an area (see Figure 2-12).

Figure 2-12 *Marker quick strokes.*

> **TIP** Customize the tip of a dry marker by cutting various patterns, notches, or slices into the tip with a utility knife. This technique provides numerous texture-making options.

> **TIP** To help bring a dry marker that still has pigment back to life, try adding a few drops or soaking the tip in rubbing alcohol for alcohol-based markers or xylene for xylene-based markers. Cap the marker and store upside down until the alcohol or xylene has been absorbed.

Turn-tip lines. This technique is used for creating a variable line or a thick or thin line, which is typically used for making the veins in marble and the grains in wood. This technique uses a freehand style, meaning that no drafting equipment, such as a straight edge, is necessary to create the line. This line results from a special way the pencil or pen is held and how much pressure is exerted by the hand.

1. *Marker turn-tip.* Using a broad- or thin-tip marker (depending on the scale of the line needed), pull and roll the marker between your fingers as marks are being made on the paper. Also, vary your hand pressure on the marker from very light to hard. The final results will be a thick, thin, or variable line that looks like the veins in marble (see Figure 2-13).

2. *Pencil turn-tip.* Hold the pencil at its tip with your index finger and thumb at an angle. Roll the tip between these fingers changing the angle of the pencil as marks are being made (see Figure 2-14).

> **TIP** When rendering marble, make sure that the marble veins vary in direction and size. Marble grains run from very fine to very thick in size and also go in numerous directions. Think of marble grains as tree branches that are growing in all directions. The opposite of this is the grains in

Figure 2-13 *Marker turn-tip technique.*

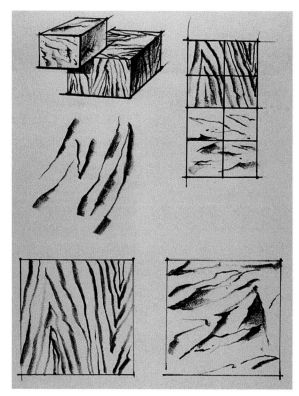

Figure 2-14 *Pencil turn-tip*

wood, where the grains run in the same direction and in a series of peaks that graduate in size.

Shaky lines. The shaky- or jagged-line technique is also a freehanded technique that is used to create the grains in wood and to simulate fabric patterns. The line will have rows of slight curling or jagged marks. The final line looks like a heartbeat line as indicated on a pulse-monitoring machine used in the medical field. Because the line is drawn freehand, the line can be bent and curved to match whatever material is being rendered (see Figure 2-15a).

T I P | The shaky-line technique can be varied in scale and curling style to represent various wood types. To indicate a wood that has a very prominent grain, such as oak, the line curls must be spread out and larger in scale. For a tighter-grained wood, such as mahogany, the line curls must be tighter and smaller in scale.

BLB lines. BLB is the acronym for *blob line blob*. BLB lines are used for outlining. The BLB technique gives a sketchy, looser look to the line work. This line technique begins and ends with a mark that resembles a blob or dot. To create this type of line with markers,

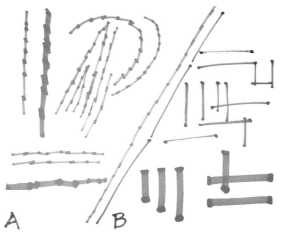

Figure 2-15 *(a) Shaky lines and (b) BLB lines.*

let the marker sit for a second to spread out or run the color into a small blob before proceeding with the line. At the end of the line, make another blob similar to the mark at the beginning.

This kind of line can also be created using a pencil. For the blob parts of the line, scrub the pencil point against the drawing surface until a point or blob is created.

The scale of blobs varies with the scale of the line. Most blobs should be about twice the size of the line (see Figure 2-15b).

Dark and light lines. This line technique is most commonly used to define the angle of light that is hitting the grout or mortar between tiles and bricks. This technique requires that a dark line be drawn next to a light line in the grout or mortar area of the

tiles or bricks. The dark line represents the shadow created by the brick or tile. Typically, if you assume the light is coming from a 45-degree angle, the dark line should appear on the right and bottom edges of brick or tile. The light line represents the light hitting the brick and normally shows on the top and left edges of the brick. The darkest and brightest lines are usually closest to the light source or to the viewer (see Figure 2-16).

T I P | When dark and light lines meet in an intersection, such as on a grid for tiles, they should never cross.

Diagonal lines. Once the surface color and details have been completed, diagonal lines are added to eliminate a flat or lifeless appear-

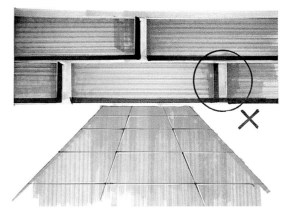

Figure 2-16 *Dark and light lines.*

ance of an object or area. Diagonal lines are of the same color but of a darker value than the surface color. To create the darker value and good transition, repeat the same color two to three times in the same location until the darker value appears. Diagonal lines are located arbitrarily across the object in thick and thin widths (see Figure 2-17).

Dots: Another technique that unifies the rendering and also adds life or interest is the inclusion of dots. Dots, similar to diagonal lines, are arbitrarily added using varying point widths. Dots can be in any color or in black or white to add interest and visual value change to a drawing. They can be applied using ink pens, pencils, and/or markers. They are added as the final touch to a rendering after all the color application and details have been completed (see Figure 2-18).

 Do not go dot crazy during application. Dots should only enhance your drawing and not interfere with the overall look of the rendering. Dots should not look like bugs all over your drawing.

Color techniques

There are several basic concepts for color application to keep in mind while rendering. The first step before applying color is to visualize what atmosphere will be created and how all the spaces and objects will relate to this atmosphere. Render with the entire environment in mind and not just one isolated object.

The color rendering of an object does not have to be an exact duplicate of the colors or materials on your material sample board. This is because there is a very different visual effect between holding the materials flat in front of you and how they will appear on the board or installed in real life. Also, there are numerous variables that can affect how a material is viewed, for instance, the type and direction of the light source, hue, color saturation, and the perspective view.

The interaction of color plays a significant role in giving character to a rendering in this book. To help achieve this character, there are basically four color concepts that must be studied. These include color-near, color-overlap, color-select, and color-white.

Color-near.   *Color-near* is a technique in which colors from surrounding objects and

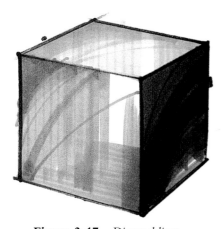

Figure 2-17   *Diagonal lines.*

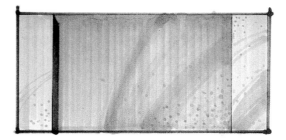

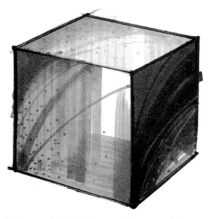

Figure 2-18   *Diagonal lines and dots.*

the immediate area are added to the object or area being rendered. For example, if the walls surrounding an object are red, then the object needs a hint of red added, even though it is another color. These splashes of color tie everything together, giving the rendering a reflective quality and adding a mysterious look to it.

The color-near technique must be added in such a way as to not overtake or interfere with the actual colors of the objects being rendered. Color-near should only read as a splash of color. Good places to add this are in the darker value areas and the edges of objects (see Figure 2-19).

Color-overlap. When applying color, let the colors close to the area being rendered overlap or bleed together. This technique, referred to as *overlap,* gives the rendering a looser appearance and value change (see Figure 2-20). Also, the color-overlapping technique can be used with different colors, thus adding new colors to a marker set which cannot be purchased. Because markers make transparent marks, when a new color is added on top of another color, the two blend together creating a new color. Use the same process as identified in the overlap technique, applying the same color as outlined above, but in step two add a different color (see Figure 2-21).

Color-select. Prior to beginning your drawing, determine how many different colors are needed. All materials in a rendering are a product of a variety of colors and their values, and not just one solid color. For example, to render wood, do not use only one brown color, but three to four values and shades of brown or yellow-oranges to create the correct wood tones. Nothing in a rendering is comprised of just one color (see Figure 2-22).

Figure 2-19 *The color-near technique.*

Color-white. Color-white is a technique in which a white space is left blank on the corner or edge of the brightest side or lightest-

Figure 2-20 *Single-marker color-overlap and use of marker as a blender.*

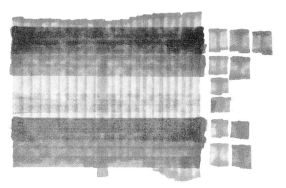

Figure 2-21 *Mixing colors with the overlap technique.*

Figure 2-22 *The color-select technique.*

value face of the object. This white area produces a high-contrast region within the object. This area is typically closest to the viewer (see the cube image in Figure 2-18).

Creating value changes with different mediums

To be able to create appropriate value changes is one of the basic skills in rendering. Establish a good foundation in color rendering by experimenting with how different values change, using pencils on basic shapes such as cylinders, boxes, cones, and spheres. This is a very beneficial exercise in your study of rendering. The cylinder, box, cone, and sphere are the most common geometric shapes typically found in constructed environments. Every object in a constructed environment evolves from one or more, or at least parts, of these shapes: the cylinder, translating into a column or a flower vase; the box, transforming into a tabletop or a sofa cushion; the sphere, becoming a planter; and the cone, changing into a wall sconce (light). Once you master how to value basic shapes, this knowledge can very easily be transferred to any object found in a constructed environment.

TIP Before beginning to render any object, analyze which geometric shapes make up the object. Forget that you are about to render a table, chair, or whatever. Instead, pretend that you are about to render several geometric shapes that, when put together, will create that object. For instance, a tabletop is a box and each round table leg is a cylinder.

Creating value changes using pencils on basic shapes
Figures 2-23 to 2-25 visually illustrate the steps which were taken in using pencils to render basic shapes.

Step 1: First establish the direction at which the light source is hitting the object. In rendering, the recommended light source hits the object on the left side at a 45-degree angle.

Next start to create value zones using the pencil. Define each side or area of the object as it relates to the light source. The side of the object or area facing the light source should be given the lightest value. The side next to the light source area should be given a medium value, and the side or area farthest away from the light source should be the darkest in value. The shadow or area behind the object should go from a dark to light value, which represents the change in distance in the plan.

Step 2: Figure 2-24 moves in depth into the three-dimensionality of each object and explores the value changes in a single object or area on an object. For example, even on

Figure 2-23 *Creating value change using pencils on basic shapes, step 1.*

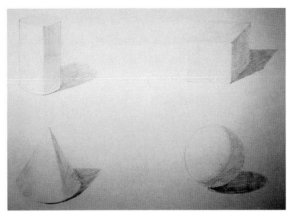

Figure 2-24 *Creating value change using pencils on basic shapes, step 2.*

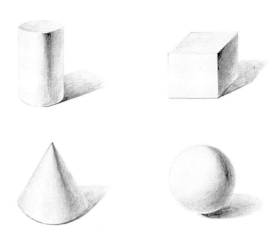

Figure 2-25 *Creating value change using pencils on basic shapes, step 3.*

the light side there should be highlights including bright spots fading to a medium value. On the dark side there should be darker spots graduating to a medium value as well as clear transitional spaces between dark and light areas.

Step 3: In general, the third step is to enhance the high-contrast areas on the object and create reflection to enhance the three-dimensionality. Contrast areas are usually on the area closest to the light source, and reflection areas are usually on the lower corner of the dark side of the object (see Figure 2-25).

 Never draw the details first. Establish each side's value and the shadows first. All sides and the shadow should

relate to each other in some degree of value. Always draw light, and then gradually get darker.

TIP You can use a straight edge when drawing the dark areas following the shape of the objects. For the reflection area you can use an eraser with an eraser shield to clean up and define the edges of reflections. The angled lines can be used for making the transitions from the dark to the highlight spots.

TIP A blender pencil and/or blender marker are excellent for smoothing out pencil marks when an even spread of value is necessary.

TIP The line technique needed to define the edges of the cube is lift-stroke. Using a straight edge, draw a line by pushing hard then gradually lifting the pencil up as the line ends. The end results should be a line that starts out dark, then gradually lightens.

Creating value changes using markers
There are basically three sets of gray-tone markers available that can be used to study value change: cool gray, warm gray, and French gray. The cool-gray set has a colder and white or gray cast; the warm grays have a purple cast; and the French-gray set appears more in the brown or sepia gray range. The lightness or darkness of the gray is indicated with a percentage: the lower the percentage,

the lighter the gray; and the higher the percentage, the darker the gray. Which gray-tone marker set is selected depends on user preference and colors appropriate for that rendering.

Gray-value bar scale. Figure 2-26 demonstrates using different values of markers to generate gradations. You may follow the image to practice the value changes using several markers of the same tone. Always start with the lightest value and grade to the darkest.

> **TIP** **Organize and line up your markers on your work surface in order of their gradation from light to dark. This will help keep you organized.**

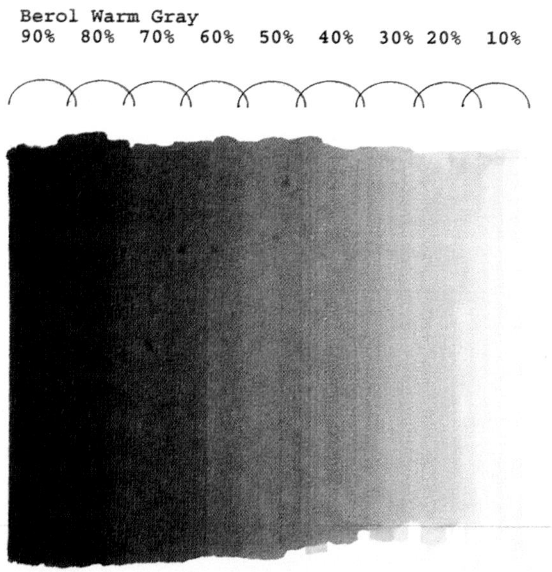

Berol Warm Gray
90% 80% 70% 60% 50% 40% 30% 20% 10%

Figure 2-26 *Gradation of markers.*

> **TIP** **To create the look of metal, start the lightest area of markers in the middle of the drawing and gradually add the darker colors (as outlined in the preceding steps), radiating from the center with the light to dark values. This technique also works well for rendering a cylinder.**

Overlapping technique with the same color. Another method of increasing the value of the depth is to overlap the same color of marker three times, but change the direction of the marks. Be sure to wait until the previous step has dried before beginning the next step.

Step 1: Create a series of vertical lines with one marker color, using a straight edge. Use an evenhanded pressure for each mark.

Step 2: Using the same marker color, add diagonal lines over the vertical ones.

Step 3: Now add, with the same marker, horizontal lines over the previously drawn vertical and diagonal ones (see Figure 2-20, *right*).

> **TIP** **Some marker colors are contaminated by using this overlapping technique. To avoid this problem, make marks on a clear piece of scrap paper after overlapping until the color marks true.**

Creating value using a blender marker. One of the quickest and easiest ways to combine the

colors of markers is to use a blender marker. The *blender marker* is composed of the base ingredient found in a color marker but minus the color pigment. When applied, the paper is saturated, causing the marker colors to run or blend together resulting in a watercolor appearance of the marks. The blender marker can be applied before or after the color marker has been applied, depending on the final results and user preference. Application of the blender and spray works best when both the marker and blender are still wet on the paper (see Figure 2-20, *left*).

It is important to keep the blender-marker tip clean to prevent previously used colors from mixing with the new colors being blended. To clean a blender-marker tip, just keep rubbing the tip on a clean piece of paper until all the color is removed from it. Some marker manufacturers provide replaceable tips for replacing worn out or dirty tips.

> **TIP** **To tone down a color, try applying the color marker to the tip of the blender marker; then use the blender to apply the color. Results will be a very light, muted color.**

Creating value changes using water-based paints

Value change with watercolor. Watercolor value change (gradation) depends on the amount of water you use on the brush. Put water on the brush up to the heel (where the bristles attach to the handle), then put color on the tip. Draw a thin line; gradually the line will become lighter because the water is coming down from the heel of the brush, thus thinning out the paint. If you want a broad stroke, use the side of the brush to draw the line. There will be a value change from dark (from the tip of the brush) to light (from the heel of the brush; see Figure 2-27a).

Value change with gouache. For paint gradation, mix one darker color with a lighter color. The gradation of color depends on the amount of each color mixed. One advantage to paint is that if the change is too dramatic, you can go back and make it smoother while it is still wet (see Figure 2-27b).

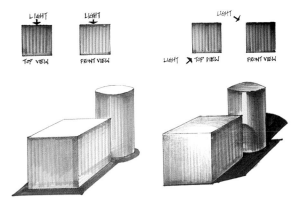

Figure 2-27 *Gradation of (a) watercolor; and (b) gouache.*

Shadow Casting and Highlighting

Shade and shadow

Shade and shadow are very important elements in successful color renderings. They particularly help us to develop a strong sense of three-dimensionality. We should not treat shade and shadow as a secondary element, but part of the initial creation of the drawing. Figure 2-28 shows the relationship of lighting, direction, and shadow when we render objects or interior spaces. If we render an object that has a light shining on it from the front and above, there should be a value of light, medium, dark, plus shade and a shadow on the object. The ability to separate these four different values is the key to three-dimensionality. The top of the object should have some white, particularly in the corner closest to you

Figure 2-28 *Shadow casting.*

and the viewer. The corner should be the strongest contrast. If you render a cylinder, the front curve should be much stronger.

The images of shade and shadow not only help us to visualize three-dimensionality, but help us to understand distance both vertically and horizontally (see Figure 2-29). You can see the difference between the shadow on the floor and on the box made by the top of the table. The shadow on the floor is much weaker than the shadow on the box. This is because the box is higher than the floor, so the shadow will be stronger. You can see that the first block of the four blocks has a very strong contrast and dark shadows, and as the distance increases, the shadow gets lighter and the contrast is reduced.

Highlighting

Highlighting on box
Before you draw, observe where the highlight will be on the object. If the highlight will fall

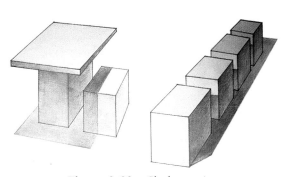

Figure 2-29 *Shadow casting.*

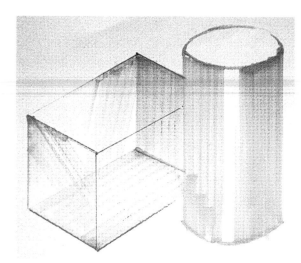

Figure 2-30   *The study of highlights on geometric shapes, step 1.*

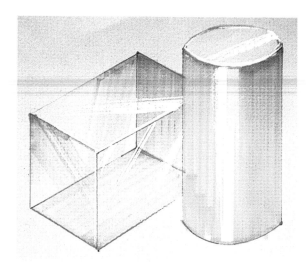

Figure 2-31   *The study of highlights on geometric shapes, step 2.*

on a flat surface, such as the top of a box, the highlight usually is represented by diagonal lines. Begin by using a basic color to cover the object. Be sure to apply the concept of gradation to the highlighted side of the box. Gradually move from light to dark. After you use markers to separate all sides of the box, use a white colored pencil to draw the highlight. Use the colored pencil to make it intense; push hard, then fade out. This technique, referred to previously in this chapter, is called the lift-stroke. Make sure the high-

contrast areas are closest to you, which is the corner of the box (see the images of the box in Figures 2-30 and 2-31).

Highlighting on cylinder
The highlights on a cylinder should be vertical. After you have identified where the highlighted spot should be, note that it should only be one-fourth of the total surface. Using a light color, start on both sides of the highlighted area you have saved and work from light to dark. Be sure the darkest

area is not on the edge of the cylinder but one-fourth of the way in from its right edge. After you smooth the transition from light to dark, use a white colored pencil and a ruler to accent the edge of the highlighted area. Start at the top of the cylinder; push hard, and then fade out. Generally, when you use a dark-toned paper for a background, it is easier to represent the highlight or any type of light. White backgrounds or white paper will not show the highlight (see the images of the cylinder in Figures 2-30 and 2-31).

Chapter 3

Rendering Basic Building Materials and Their Finishes

This chapter demonstrates how to render several commonly used materials in architectural and interior environments. The examples focus on mixing the rendering mediums to create the desired finish or surface effect. Attention is directed to the ease and speed with which the materials can be recreated. The basic techniques, demonstrated in the previous chapter, are applied in the renderings.

General Steps for Color Rendering

1. *The total impression of the object or the environment.* Before you render, take time to extract the essence of a space or an object without too much analytical thinking about the structure and its details. Do not just think about what it looks like, but rather, visualize the atmosphere you want to create. Always consider the entire surrounding environment, not just the one isolated object.

2. *Apply colors and create basic structure.* Many objects and spaces are composed of very simple geometric shapes. By looking at the point where the light meets the dark side of the object, you may determine your *drawing color palette,* which is a group of markers and color pencils that include light, medium, and dark, plus one even darker color for the shadow. Prior to beginning your drawing, determine the number and colors of markers required. For example, to render wood use three to four browns or yellow-oranges to create the color. For a black color, you might use layers of medium to dark gray, and finally black. Never expect to use one magic color to represent your material. The color rendering of your object does not have to be an exact duplication of the material or color on the finished board because there is a very different visual effect between holding the material flat in front of you and how it will appear on the board or installed in the actual environment.

There are numerous variables which affect the way a material is seen, such as light, distance, hue, color saturation, and perspective. At this stage, drawing should be done in a loose style. Use very quick strokes with the broad edge of the marker to define the three-dimensionality of the object and give it the basic color. Always leave white space (color-white technique) on the corner or edge of the bright side of the object nearest the light source. This area will later become a high-contrast region. This field is visually closest to you.

3. *Rendering the details.* Render the structures, textures, and three-dimensionality. At this stage, the drawing style is probably a little tighter. Use various drawing techniques as introduced in previous chapters. Use the flat and pointed tip of the marker along with different sides of the pencil.

4. *Environmental effects on the object.* At this stage, think about reflections and color interaction and how the effects of distance change the color intensity. After the surface color and detail have been applied to the object or space, it may appear flat or lifeless. Using diagonal lines and several dots may add some life to the object, and providing reflections of other colors around the object using the color-near technique will tie everything together. The drawing style at this level should be a little looser than in the previous stage.

5. *Unify the rendering.* During steps 2 and 3, you may have been so focused on one object or one area in the space that you forgot about how it relates to other objects within the space. Expand your vision to the whole shape or space. In this step, you may want to eliminate some detail you have drawn to better suit the whole picture. For example, a table in the background may have too much detail and stand out too much, so you may want to eliminate that contrast.

Materials and Finishes

Marble

Because colored pencils are easily controlled, use this medium first to render a marble cylinder and to help you understand the rendering process. Also, it becomes easier to make the transition from colored pencils to other mediums, such as markers or watercolors. You may follow the Figures 3-1 to 3-3 as an experiment using pencils to render a marble cylinder.

A gray marble cube
Before you draw, analyze the three-dimensionality of the object you are going to

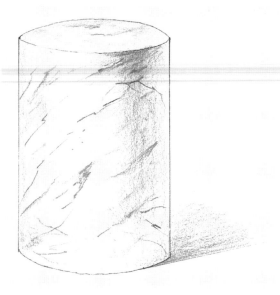

Figure 3-2 *Using colored pencils to draw a marble cylinder, step 2.*

Figure 3-1 *Using colored pencils to draw a marble cylinder, step 1.*

Figure 3-3 *Using colored pencils to draw a marble cylinder, step 3.*

render. Study pictures of marble or an actual sample of the marble you want to represent. Then select appropriate colors for the rendering. In general, start with the marker first because you can put pencil over marker, but you cannot easily cover pencil with marker.

With the broad edge of a light-gray-color marker, make quick vertical strokes. Add the base color to the cube face and right side. The face will be lighter than the right side, so press hard when you draw the right side. Make sure to be loose. On the top side, use diagonal lines with a quick stroke to apply a base color. Always leave some white on the front and top sides, particularly around the corner which appears closest to you (see Figure 3-4).

With the light-gray marker, use a quick stroke to apply another layer of color on an area that you have previously drawn to replicate the variations on the surface. Then, with the turn-tip technique, use the same marker to put in the veining on the front and top of the cube. Apply more color to the face using the same marker and doing the various strokes with different tips. The marble grain flows in different directions and is naturally structured with texture; as a result, some marble lines are thin, some are thick, some blend, and some crack. Therefore, your marker strokes should go in various directions and be applied with multiple line techniques (see Figure 3-5).

Continue to use the light-gray marker to add some veining on the top of the cube to show the change of value created by the marble grain and cracks. Then use the second marker, which is a little darker than the first marker (the light-gray marker), to apply another layer of color on the top of the cube and to some areas on the front and side. Also, use the second marker to add some darker grain on top of the previously rendered areas but do not cover all the areas, only the deeper cracks (see Figure 3-6).

Start to introduce the third-darkest marker, and add some veining to all three sides. So far, we have been using the broad edge of the marker. Now, change to the fine tip and add some clearer lines, organizing the grains or veins. Use light blue to add some color to the right half of the front side (see Figure 3-7).

Using the fourth-darkest marker and the fine tip, add some darker veining. Start using several line techniques which were introduced in Chapter 2, such as shaky-line, jagged, and BLB, to provide the variation in

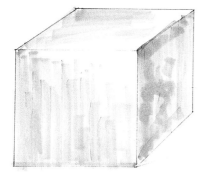

Figure 3-4 *Gray marble cube, step 1.*

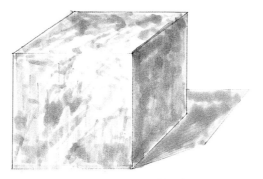

Figure 3-5 *Gray marble cube, step 2.*

Figure 3-6 *Gray marble cube, step 3.*

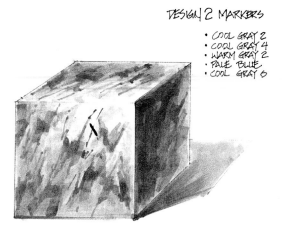

DESIGN 2 MARKERS
• COOL GRAY 2
• COOL GRAY 4
• WARM GRAY 2
• PALE BLUE
• COOL GRAY 6

Figure 3-7   *Gray marble cube, step 4.*

the marble grains. Then use the broad edge of the marker to add a layer of color to the right side. Touch up the shadow by increasing the darkness in its front part (see Figure 3-8).

Use the fine tip of the darkest-gray marker to clean up the veining and the edges. Add increasingly more solid color on the top of the left side to make sure that the top-right corner is the area of highest contrast. Start to use colored pencils to clean up the edges and to create some sharper lines and deeper cracks. On the dark side, use sharper light pencils, such as light gray and blue, to draw some veins representing the reflection. On the light side of the cube, use a dark colored pencil, such as dark blue and gray, to define several marble grains and a couple deeper cracks. Also, you may use the side of a pencil to draw a reflection on the rear of the dark side to increase the sense of distance from the high-contrast corner to the lower-right corner on the dark side (see Figure 3-9).

At this stage, you can make the cube look similar to tile. Use your ink pen first to draw dark divided lines, then use white pencil to draw highlights on the top and left side of each tile. Remember the tiles have grout in between, so one side of the grout will be lighter than the other, depending on your light source (see Figure 3-10). Never cross the highlight and the shadow on the grout. (Refer to the dark and light line technique discussed in Chapter 2. Also, another option is to use a white ink pen instead of a white colored pencil.)

White marble cylinder
First draw the basic color and separate the different values on the cylinder.

Use the broad edge of a light marker with quick strokes to apply a coat of color. Be sure

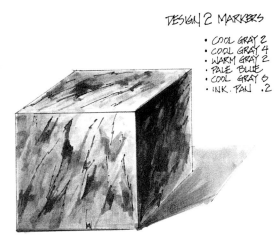

DESIGN 2 MARKERS
• COOL GRAY 2
• COOL GRAY 4
• WARM GRAY 2
• PALE BLUE
• COOL GRAY 6
• INK PAN .2

Figure 3-8   *Gray marble cube, step 5.*

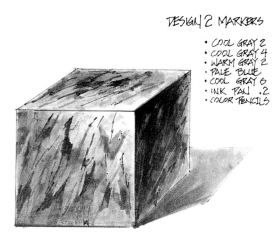

DESIGN 2 MARKERS
• COOL GRAY 2
• COOL GRAY 4
• WARM GRAY 2
• PALE BLUE
• COOL GRAY 6
• INK PAN .2
• COLOR PENCILS

Figure 3-9   *Gray marble cube, step 6.*

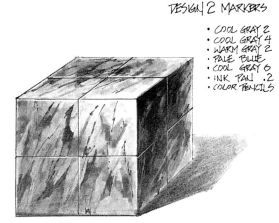

DESIGN 2 MARKERS
• COOL GRAY 2
• COOL GRAY 4
• WARM GRAY 2
• PALE BLUE
• COOL GRAY 6
• INK PAN .2
• COLOR PENCILS

Figure 3-10   *Gray marble cube, step 7.*

to leave a white stripe located on one-third of the left side of the cylinder for the highlighted area. Use the same marker to go over the right side of the cylinder to establish the dark side. Press your marker hard and move slowly to draw a couple lines one-third in from the right edge of the cylinder for the dark band. This should be the darkest area on the entire cylinder. Then, using the turn-tip technique, put in veining on all sides (see Figure 3-11).

With the second- and third-darkest markers, use the fine tip employing the shaky-line and turn-tip techniques to make the veining crisper. At the same time, organize and clean up some veinings. Use the third-darkest marker to go over the upper part of the darkest area to increase the contrast. The lower part of the cylinder has some reflection from the flat surface, so it should not be as dark as the upper part (see Figure 3-12).

Use two to three gray colored pencils to make jagged lines for more veinings. One or two cracks can be very dark. Use dark-gray pencil to draw a shadow on the bottom of the highlight area on the cylinder and the closest area on the shadow (see Figure 3-13).

Marble in a cone shape
You may follow the same procedure used to render the marble cylinder to complete this study (see Figures 3-14, 3-15, and 3-16).

Figure 3-11 *White marble cylinder, step 1.*

Figure 3-12 *White marble cylinder, step 2.*

Figure 3-13 *White marble cylinder, step 3.*

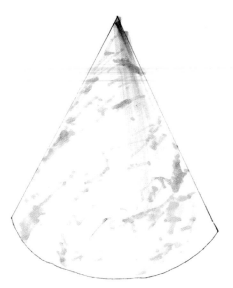

Figure 3-14   *White marble cone, step 1.*

COOL GRAY 2
COLOR PENCILS

Figure 3-15   *White marble cone, step 2.*

Figure 3-16   *White marble cone, step 3.*

Wood

Cherry wood

Use the broad edge of a light wood-colored marker to apply a layer of color to all sides of the cube. Draw twice on the right side to provide the changed amount of value compared to the other two sides. Leave a white highlighted area on the face and top of the cube (see Figure 3-17).

Use the fine tip of the lighter hue and the medium hue of the dark wood markers to draw wood grain on all sides of the cube, but the direction of the grain on each side should be different. Do not draw the grain in straight lines but go slowly, creating jagged lines (see Figure 3-18).

Use the broad edge of a red wood-colored marker to add some red tones. Try one more dark wood-colored marker to cover the dark

Figure 3-18   *Cherry wood block, step 2.*

side of the cube, particularly close to the high-contrast corner. Use the fine tip to clean up the edges. Also, add the shadow at this point (see Figure 3-19).

Go over the drawing with a couple of brown colored pencils to refine and empha-

size some wood grains and sharpen the edges. Remember to leave the white near the highlight area.

Using light-brown and medium-yellow colored pencils, draw some wood grains on the dark side of the cube. Apply a few strokes of dark-brown and red colored pencil to simulate the wood grain on the light side. Use dark marker or pencil to sharpen the primary shadow, making it darker toward the front of the shadow. Finally, use a sharp white colored pencil to highlight the edges on the front side. Using the lift-stroke technique, which was explained in Chapter 2, draw the white lines, which should start at the corner and then lead outward (see Figure 3-20).

All wood types can be done using the same techniques and employing the same percentages that were used to render cherry

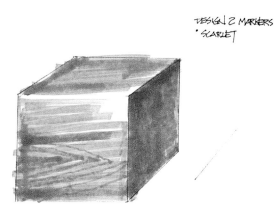

Figure 3-17   *Cherry wood block, step 1.*

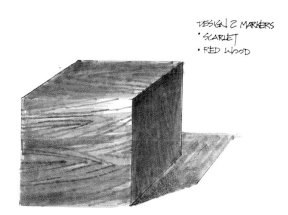

Figure 3-19   *Cherry wood block, step 3.*

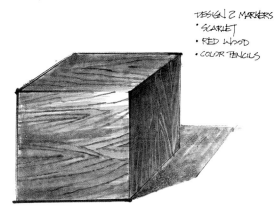

Figure 3-20   *Cherry wood block, step 4.*

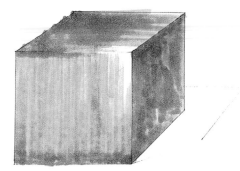

Figure 3-21   *Mahogany wood block, step 1.*

Figure 3-22   *Mahogany wood block, step 2.*

Figure 3-23   *Mahogany wood block, step 3.*

wood. Just change the colors for the appropriate type of wood.

Mahogany

As previously noted, you may use a similar percentage as that used in rendering cherry wood.

Apply two layers of color to the face of the cube. On the right side, make the area darker. On the top, make the back edge and left edge darker and lighten the stroke as you go in toward the highlight area (see Figure 3-21).

Employ the fine tip of the medium hue and the more intense hue of the dark-brown markers to begin adding the grain, using the jagged-line technique (see Figure 3-22).

Use the more intense dark wood marker to go over the right side, with the exception of the lower and back areas. Introduce the fourth and most intense dark wood color to define the grain, clean the edges, and go over the top-left corner on the dark side (see Figure 3-23).

Use a dark-brown colored pencil to fix the grain and a light colored pencil to provide reflections. Use white pencil to clean up and sharpen the edges (see Figure 3-24).

Figures 3-25 and 3-26 demonstrate the process of rendering light oak wood.

DESIGN 2 MARKERS
• BROWN OCHRE
• CHOCOLATE
• SCARLET

DESIGN 2 MARKERS
• ORANGE VALUE 1
• YELLOW ORANGE VALUE 5

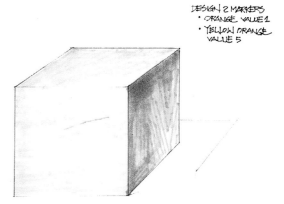

Figure 3-25 *Light oak wood block, step 1.*

Figure 3-24 *Mahogany wood block, step 4.*

DESIGN 2 MARKERS
• ORANGE VALUE 1
• YELLOW ORANGE VALUE 5
• COLOR PENCILS

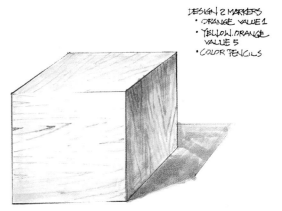

Figure 3-26 *Light oak wood block, step 2.*

Stones

Stone block

Use the broad edge of a light, warm-gray marker to separate the three sides. Then use the same marker and another medium-warm gray to draw individual pieces of stone of varied sizes (see Figure 3-27).

The rough surface of stone is not just one color but consists of several changes in value. Use the same light marker to go over some pieces and clean up edges, following along the outer shape. The texture of stone is not even, so do not apply your marker with even pressure (see Figure 3-28).

Assume that the light comes from a 45-degree angle, then add shadows below. Use the fine tip of several markers to clean up the edges of a few pieces of stone on the stone block. The dark line should show on the bottom and right side of stone. Add one more dark color on the entire dark side. Use the jagged-line technique on the front side and top, making big blotches instead of veining to create stone texture (see Figure 3-29).

Choose the colored pencils that match your marker color and give texture to the blotches of color. Use colored pencils to define several pieces that are close to the high-contrast corner on the front side. Use a very dark marker to underline the box (see Figure 3-30).

Figures 3-31 and 3-32 are examples of some other colors found in rough stone. You

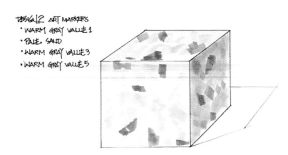

Figure 3-27 *Light color stone block, step 1.*

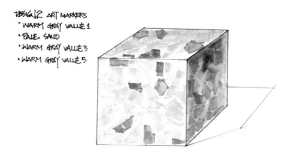

Figure 3-28 *Light color stone block, step 2.*

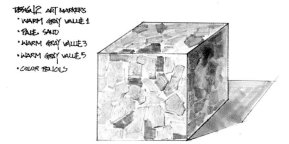

Figure 3-29 *Light color stone block, step 3.*

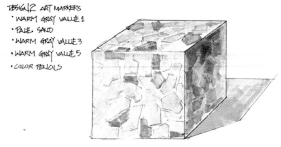

Figure 3-30 *Light color stone block, step 4.*

Figure 3-31 *Dark color stone block, step 1.*

Figure 3-32 *Dark color stone block, step 2.*

may follow the procedure previously described, using a different choice of colors.

Rough-cut stone
Figures 3-33, 3-34, and 3-35 demonstrate the steps for drawing rough-cut stones with two different kinds of rough surfaces. Start constructing the facade with variously sized pieces, filling in the basic color of the stone. Then, depending on the type of stone, create blotches on each piece. Use both the broad and fine tips of the markers to draw the bumps. The smooth surface should have less contrast than the rough surface. Rough-cut stone makes shadows, so add a dark line on the bottom and right side of several pieces. Finally, use a dark colored pencil to show the division between stones. Use several colored pencils, which should include bright, medium, and dark colors, to enhance the bumpy surface of the stone.

Figure 3-33   *Rough-cut stone, step 1.*

Figure 3-35   *Rough-cut stone, step 3.*

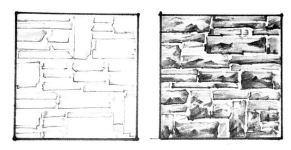

Figure 3-34   *Rough-cut stone, step 2.*

Masonry block

Render one layer of light gray on all sides. Then, using a darker gray marker, draw lines to divide the block so they are in a concrete blocklike arrangement. Use colored pencil to clean up the lines. Use the side of medium- and light-gray pencils to give some rough texture to the surfaces. Stipple with a darker marker and colored pencil. Draw various value dots on the blocks (see Figure 3-36).

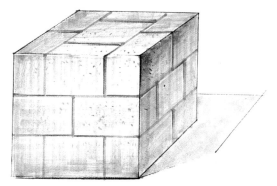

Figure 3-36   *Masonry blocks.*

Glass blocks

Once again, before you begin drawing, analyze the structure to figure out what the main characteristics are. Glass block has a certain thickness and is not as transparent as flat glass. First, use a warm light gray to draw a square, then divide it into four panels, and use the broad edge of the marker to quickly give the blocks thickness. Next, with the same marker, use very short strokes going in different directions to draw the surface of the glass block. Use the fine tip of the marker to better con-

struct the shape of the blocks. Assume the light is coming from above and to the left. The sides of the block will have the shade and the shadow (see Figure 3-37). In the next stage employ two more dark markers in the same light-brown tones plus a colored pencil. Use the markers to give depth and variety to the glass block surface. Keep using different strokes in a variety of directions. Also, start refining each block individually. The two pieces closest to you should show more detail, and the blocks closest to you will exhibit the highest contrast along the edge (see Figure 3-38).

Figure 3-37   *Glass block, step 1.*

Figure 3-38   *Glass block, step 2.*

Use the straight-edged ruler with color pencils for cleaning up the edges, and put another layer of color on the side nearest to you. Sketch white, short diagonal lines on the surface for the feeling of transparence (see Figure 3-39).

T I P Let the color absorb into the paper to help show the texture of the glass block.

Figure 3-39 *Glass block, step 3.*

Brick

The detailed explanation and illustrations of the rendering process for bricks are included in the section entitled "Visual Comparison of Four Different Mediums" later in this chapter.

Textiles

It is very challenging to render textiles because it is not just a flat surface that is involved but the textiles' surface textures and patterns. Normally, markers can be used for giving the basic color, the folding pleats, and the pattern of the textile. Colored pencils are important tools for providing texture.

Iridescent textile

Study the characteristics of the textile and consider what colors can be used to achieve that particular surface composition. Select a group of markers and colored pencils that will express the texture. You can use any removable tape to cover the edge of the drawing area. Then, when you are done rendering, you can pull the tape off, leaving the clean edge of the drawing (see Figure 3-40).

First, use a light marker to give the feeling of the textile. How does it fold and bend? Where are the shades and shadows, and what is the main pattern involved? In this case, it is yellow leaves (see Figure 3-41). The next step is to give the basic color of the textile and make sure the textile is not viewed as flat. There should be texture and pattern created by using the markers in different directions. The area close to the folds should bend toward the direction of the fold. For the other flat areas, use a variety of long and short lines in all different directions (see Figure 3-42).

Now, increase the three-dimensionality and the fluidity of the folding area. Use dark colors to represent the shadow and use a medium

Figure 3-40   *Iridescent textile, step 1.*

Figure 3-41   *Iridescent textile, step 2.*

Figure 3-42   *Iridescent textile, step 3.*

Figure 3-43   *Iridescent textile, step 4.*

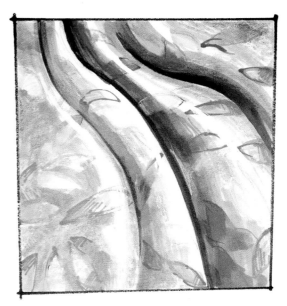

Figure 3-44   *Iridescent textile, step 5.*

color to make the transition from the shadow to the highlighted area. Only part of the pattern, which falls on the fold, is visible, so contrast that area with the flat surface where all the pattern is visible (see Figure 3-43).

The last stage is to refine more. Leave the highlighted areas and be especially aware of the highlights on the shiny textiles. Also, the pattern or flowers have a stronger contrast on the light part of the textile and less contrast on the darker area of the fabric. Use the dark color for the patterns that fall on the light area. Make sure to incorporate reflection on the dark side of the folding area. Colored pencils are very useful for this stage. Use the

tip for drawing the detail and also drawing the edge to give it texture (see Figure 3-44).

Textiles with geometric patterns and texture
Use the wide edge of the marker to define the movement of the fold and also the basic color of the textile (see Figure 3-45). Then start with the same marker, previously used, but apply short strokes with uneven pressure, similar to cross-hatching. This provides a rough-textured feeling. The dark, folded area is flatter with less contrast and shows the highlighting in the bright area more clearly. Add a second layer of dark color to give more depth to the fabric. The second color

Figure 3-45   *Textile with geometric pattern, step 1.*

Figure 3-46 *Textile with geometric pattern, step 2.*

Figure 3-47 *Textile with geometric pattern, step 3.*

highlight area, which should show strong contrast. The use of the point of a pencil for light areas and the pencil's side for the flat and shaded areas helps to develop texture. Make sure there is reflection on the dark side of each fold. Be very careful to avoid a two-dimensional, flat feeling for the folds. Instead, use different amounts of pressure with the pencil and marker, concentrating on some areas, but not all areas (see Figure 3-48).

Textile mapping on cylindrical shapes
The next study is to draw textile mapping on several cylindrical shapes. The first step is

should only be used on the shaded area and some selected flat areas (see Figure 3-46).

The next step is to draw the blue geometric lines. These lines should follow the folding movement of the fabric. The flat surface is horizontal, and the folded surface should be curved. The blue lines should help in generating the characteristics of the material (see Figure 3-47). Using the third- or fourth-darkest colors, draw on the shadowed area to increase the three-dimensionality of the folds. Then, follow with different colored pencils and the fine tip of the marker to refine. Use the fine tip of the marker to carefully refine several areas of the fabric, particularly in the

Figure 3-48 *Textile with geometric pattern, step 4.*

Figure 3-49 *Textile mapping on cylindrical shapes, step 1.*

to determine the basic color of the textile while concentrating on the fundamental characteristics of the object. The cylinder should have a highlight plus a light and dark side. The basic color and pattern of the textile shows much more clearly in the light-side area than in the dark and shade areas. In the darker area, there is a light color and the contrasts in the pattern are not strong (see Figure 3-49).

Now refine further, using the ruler and marker to give stronger contrast for each object and more detail of color and pattern along the lighter portion of the object (see Figure 3-50). In the last step, your attention is shifted back to the basic principles of rendering a cylinder. Give more contrast to the area closest to you. Provide more darkness and brightness on the front of the cylinder to add more depth to the drawing (see Figure 3-51).

Reflective Materials

Metal cube

The best way to draw metal is to use the value-change technique (gradation) with diagonal lines. Gradation is very important to represent the shininess of metal. Before starting to draw, decide where the highlight is going to be, then save a diagonal strip on the front side and top of the metal cube with differently graded angles to represent the central highlighted area on these two sides. Then use several markers to create a value gradation on all sides of the cube (see Figure 3-52).

After using several different value markers, go over each side with a light and medium color to blend the edge of the two values

Figure 3-50 *Textile mapping on cylindrical shapes, step 2.*

Figure 3-51 *Textile mapping on cylindrical shapes, step 3.*

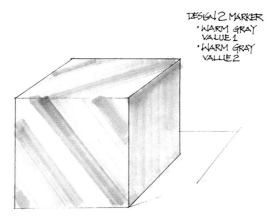

Figure 3-52 *Metal cube, step 1.*

together (see Figure 3-53). On the right side, use a medium value, perhaps a value 6, as the lightest color to use on the dark side of the cube (see Figure 3-54).

The front face should show a clearer gradation than the top that continues along the dark side (see Figure 3-55).

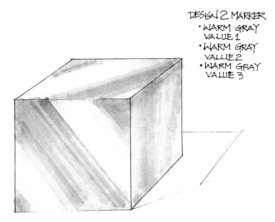

DESIGN 2 MARKER
• WARM GRAY VALUE 1
• WARM GRAY VALUE 2
• WARM GRAY VALUE 3

Figure 3-53   *Metal cube, step 2.*

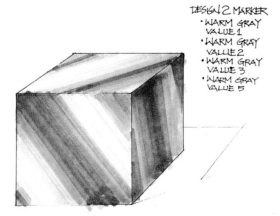

DESIGN 2 MARKER
• WARM GRAY VALUE 1
• WARM GRAY VALUE 2
• WARM GRAY VALUE 3
• WARM GRAY VALUE 5

Figure 3-54   *Metal cube, step 3.*

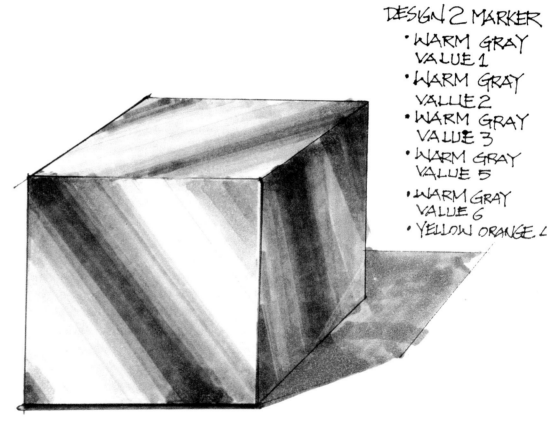

DESIGN 2 MARKER
• WARM GRAY VALUE 1
• WARM GRAY VALUE 2
• WARM GRAY VALUE 3
• WARM GRAY VALUE 5
• WARM GRAY VALUE 6
• YELLOW ORANGE L

Figure 3-55   *Metal cube, step 4.*

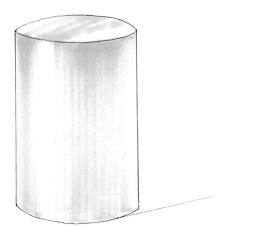

·DESIGN 2 MARKER
· ORANGE
  VALUE 1

Figure 3-56 *Metal cylinder, step 1.*

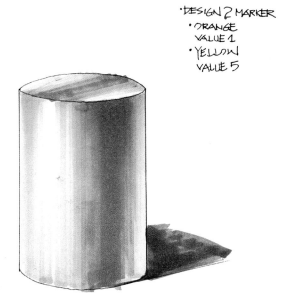

·DESIGN 2 MARKER
· ORANGE
  VALUE 1
· YELLOW
  VALUE 5

Figure 3-57 *Metal cylinder, step 2.*

Metal cylinder

Vertical lines are the best for drawing curved surfaces. Apply the first layer of color to the cylinder, leaving one stripe on the side which receives the light for a highlight area (see Figure 3-56). Add a little darker color on the right side of the cylinder. Then add a darker color on the middle of the right half (see Figure 3-57). The bottom of the shaded area shows the most reflection. It should be drawn with a really sharp line, which starts at the bottom-right edge of the cylinder and leads straight up, fading out (see Figure 3-58).

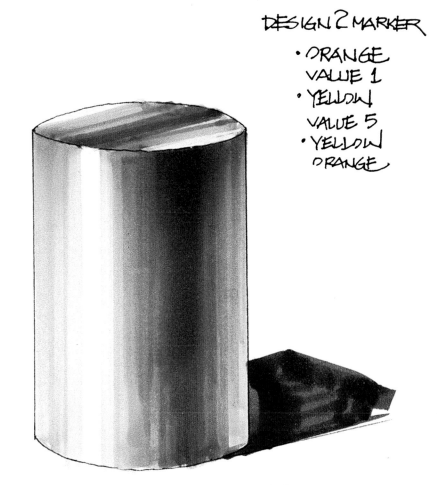

DESIGN 2 MARKER

· ORANGE
  VALUE 1
· YELLOW
  VALUE 5
· YELLOW
  ORANGE

Figure 3-58 *Metal cylinder, step 3.*

Mirror

The best way to represent a mirror is to have the actual object and the mirror image of the object appear in the same drawing (see Figure 3-59). Always render the actual objects realistically and render the image appearing in the mirror with less contrast (see Figure 3-60). After rendering the reflected object in the mirror, add white diagonal lines across the mirror to identify that the reflected object is on the flat surface of the mirror (see Figure 3-61).

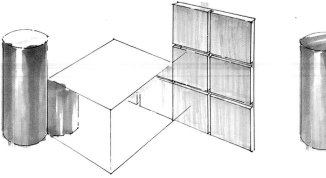

Figure 3-59   *Mirror, step 1.*

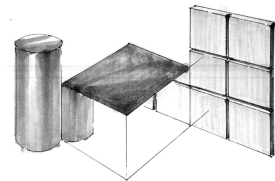

Figure 3-60   *Mirror, step 2.*

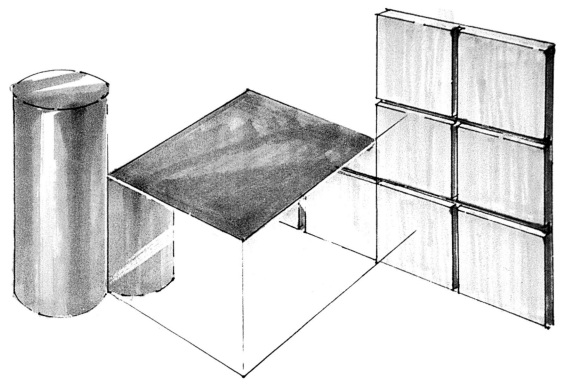

Figure 3-61   *Mirror, step 3.*

Glass cube

Use a light-blue marker with different pressures and with strokes in various directions to separate all sides of the glass block. Make sure the right side of the block is the darkest one. The diagonal lines on each panel should be in different directions (see Figure 3-62).

Next, introduce a darker blue to intensify the three-dimensionality of the boxes. Apply even firmer strokes to the dark side of the cube (see Figure 3-63).

Now use colored pencils to draw the highlight and clean up the edges. The upper-right corner on the front side should have the highest contrast. The directions of the highlights on each separate panel should be at different angles. Use the sharp tip of the pencil to draw the strong highlight and clean up the edges. Then use the side of the pencil to fade out some of the areas (see Figure 3-64).

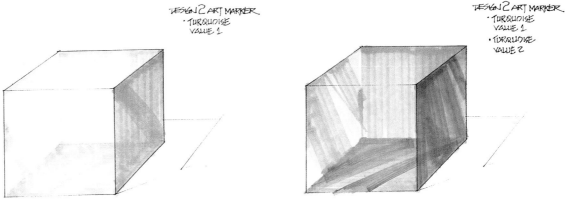

Figure 3-62   *Glass cube, step 1.*

Figure 3-63   *Glass cube, step 2.*

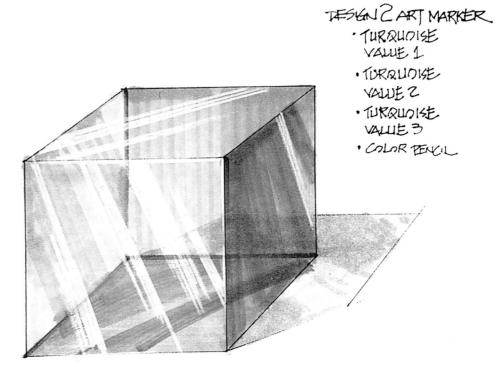

Figure 3-64   *Glass cube, step 3.*

Visual Comparison of Four Different Mediums

This section simply provides a visual presentation of the results available by using different mediums, such as markers, colored pencils, watercolors, and gouache. The material surfaces that are rendered are wood panels, marble tiles, glass, and brick. Most of the materials and mediums utilized have been well explained in previous chapters.

In this section, explanations emphasize the use of gouache to render brick. Examine the upper right-hand corner of the four blocks in Figures 3-65 through 3-69 for a demonstration of how to use gouache to draw bricks.

Figure 3-65 represents the basic color of the brick. It is not just one color, but should be a combination of the colors in the individual bricks. This may involve browns, red-

browns, reds, or dark brown. Use the brush to mix several colors together and apply quick strokes to give the basic tones of the bricks.

Figure 3-66 demonstrates how to transfer the layout of the bricks onto the area you already colored. The construction of bricks may be drawn on a separate sheet of transparent paper. On the back of the transparent paper you can put a little bit of colored pencil to give it a small amount of color. Then use the straight-edged ruler and a pencil to press hard to trace over the lines. The marker should show on the drawing area which you already washed with a brush.

Figure 3-67 illustrates how to continually use brushes to draw more detail. You should use light colors to draw the mortar lines that separate different pieces of the brick.

In Figure 3-68, use very fine brushes to follow the dark and light line technique to clean up the edges of the bricks. Assume the light is coming from a 45-degree angle on the left side. The bottom and right side of each brick should have dark shadows. A highlighted area should remain at the top and left side of the bricks. Make sure the shadows and the highlights never go across the mortar (see Figure 3-69 for detail).

Figure 3-65   *Bricks rendered by four separate mediums, step 1.*

Figure 3-66   *Bricks rendered by four separate mediums, step 2.*

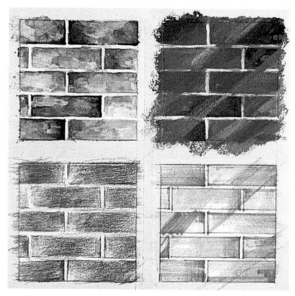

Figure 3-67   *Bricks rendered by four separate mediums, step 3.*

Figures 3-70 through 3-73 demonstrate the result of using four mediums to draw wood panels: The left square on the top was done by gouache; the right one was done by watercolor; the left one on the bottom was drawn by colored pencils; and the last was done by markers.

The next three images (Figures 3-74 through 3-76) show the steps for rendering marble tiles with different mediums. From the top left, top right, bottom left, and bottom right, the mediums are colored pencil, watercolor, gouache, and marker, respectively.

Figures 3-77 through 3-79 show the process of rendering glass, using such mediums as gouache, watercolor, colored pencil, and marker.

Figure 3-69　*Bricks rendered by four separate mediums, step 5.*

Figure 3-71　*Wood panels rendered by four separate mediums, step 2.*

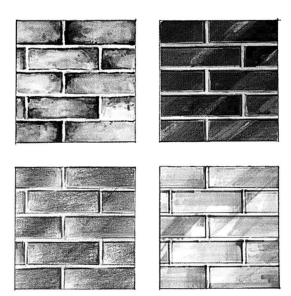

Figure 3-68　*Bricks rendered by four separate mediums, step 4.*

Figure 3-70　*Wood panels rendered by four separate mediums, step 1.*

Figure 3-72　*Wood panels rendered by four separate mediums, step 3.*

Figure 3-73 *Wood panels rendered by four separate mediums, step 4.*

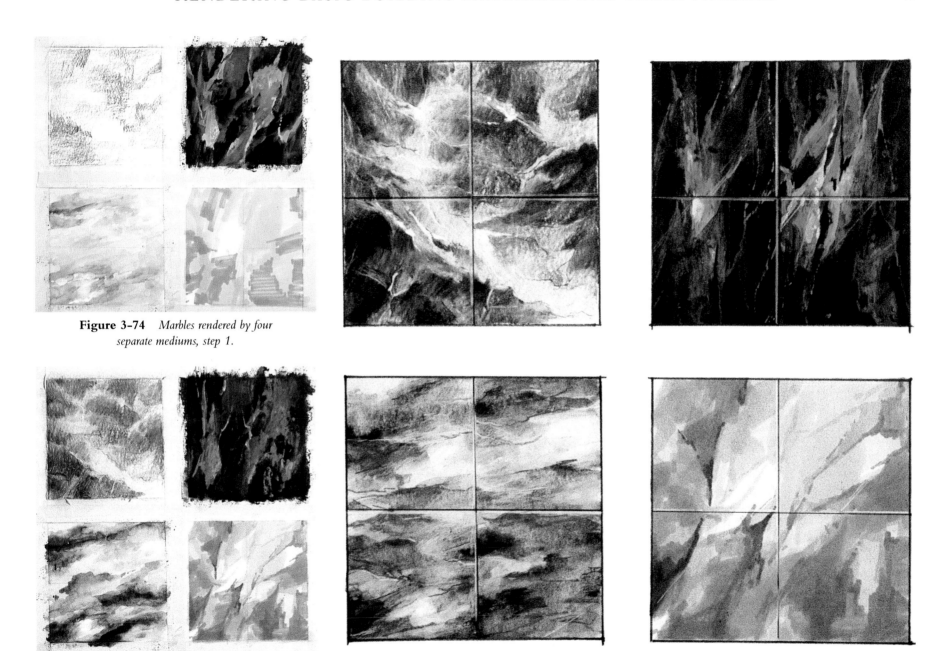

Figure 3-74 *Marbles rendered by four separate mediums, step 1.*

Figure 3-75 *Marbles rendered by four separate mediums, step 2.*

Figure 3-76 *Marbles rendered by four separate mediums, step 3.*

Figure 3-77 *Glass rendered by four separate mediums, step 1.*

Figure 3-78 *Glass rendered by four separate mediums, step 2.*

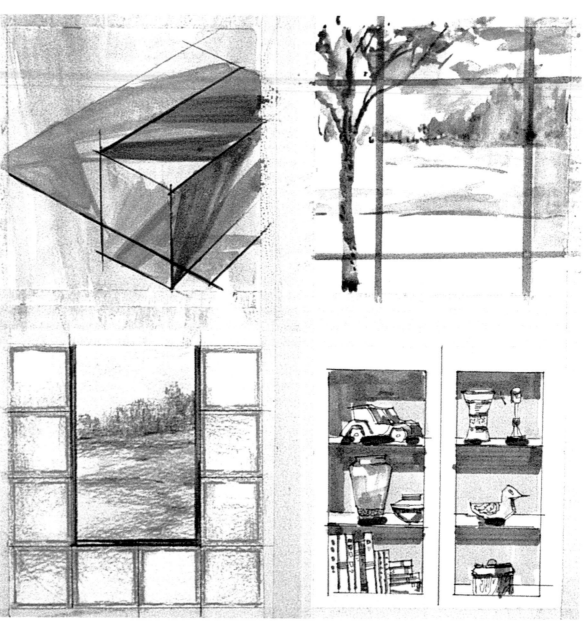

Figure 3-79 *Glass rendered by four separate mediums, step 3.*

Chapter 4

Rendering Objects and Features in Interiors

This chapter discusses sequentially how to render individual objects and design elements found in interior architectural environments. The discussion includes both residential and commercial environments, supplying one or more examples of how to render a typical object or groups of objects in various categories. Similar objects will only be illustrated without a detailed explanation. The unnarrated illustrations serve as visual reference also.

Furniture

Side chairs and armchairs

With the form and shape of the chairs in mind, use the broad edge of the markers to put on the basic color for each of the chairs. The seat and the back of chairs should not be flat. Be sure to leave some white area to be highlighted on the seat and back of the chairs. Using two gray colors and the lift-line technique, draw the metal leg structures. Provide an evenness to the metal surfaces. Even if the legs are cylindrical in shape, you should leave one side darker and make the other side bright or light gray. If the legs are square, one side should be darker than the other. Again, do not forget to leave an area for the highlight on the legs (see Figure 4-1).

Carefully shape each characteristic of the chairs with an eye for their three-dimensionality. Be sure to include strong shade and shadows on the chairs (see Figure 4-2).

The last step is to use colored pencil and the fine tip of the marker to deepen the color on the chairs. Make some more concentrated areas of color on the chairs. The right side on the red chair closest to you should have more contrasting highlights and reflections than the

Figure 4-1   *Side chairs, step 1.*

Figure 4-2   *Side chairs, step 2.*

51

Figure 4-3   *Side chair, step 3.*

Figure 4-4   *Armchair, step 1.*

Figure 4-5   *Armchair, step 2.*

Figure 4-6   *Armchair, step 3.*

chair behind it. This high-contrast area will help to establish the depth of your drawing (see Figure 4-3).

Figures 4-4 through 4-7 demonstrate how to draw different materials, textures, and the construction of the armchairs. When drawing the fabric on a chair, first keep in mind how the fabric is mapping on three-dimensional objects. The strong three-dimensional feel often is the key to successfully drawing any type of chair. Always leave some white area for the reflection area. Use a diagonal line to help make a smooth transition from dark to light, and also use the near-color technique to interrelate the colors.

Figure 4-7   *Armchair, step 4.*

Sofas

There are three different kinds of sofas represented here, and the fabrics are solid colors, geometric patterns; and floral patterns. Before you render, select a group of markers and colored pencils for each sofa. First start by giving a basic color and defining the value changes on all sides of the sofas. Always be brave enough to leave some white space for the highlight areas. When drawing a sofa, most of the time the bright area is on the seat or the armrest. When drawing the pillows, use different lines; some should be short and some long. Make sure there is a shadow on the bottom of the pillows (see Figure 4-8).

Now, work on more detail. The pattern on the object should change direction with the contours of the object. The pattern on the light area should have a stronger and clearer contrast than the darker part. Save an area for the highlight. Also, make a smooth transition from the bright highlight to the shadows (see Figure 4-9).

Finally, use colored pencils to draw the very detailed areas which are the areas closest to you. For the top sofa the detailed area is the corner of the left armrest. It should have very strong contrast. For this fabric with a floral pattern, you may want to use the side of several different colored pencils to give it the rough texture. For the middle and lower

sofas you should use colored pencil to enhance the shadows on the seat and on the armrests (see Figure 4-10).

Figures 4-11, 4-12, and 4-13 demonstrate the procedure for rendering lounge settings. The first step is to add a basic color and to think about the basic shapes of the settings.

Plants should also be considered as having dark and light sides and shadows. Once again, save white space for the highlight area on the seats and backs. When you draw textures, use both the fine point and the side of pencils.

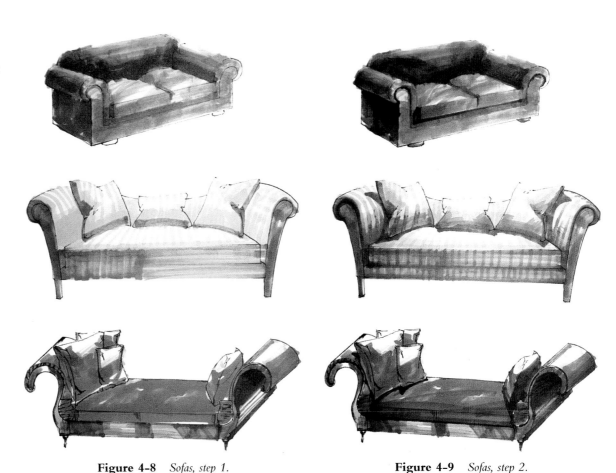

Figure 4-8 *Sofas, step 1.*   **Figure 4-9** *Sofas, step 2.*

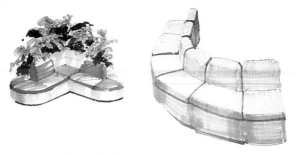

Figure 4-11 *Lounge setting, step 1.*

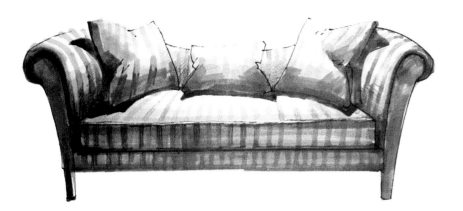

Figure 4-12 *Lounge setting, step 2.*

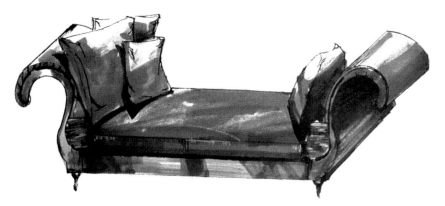

Figure 4-10 *Sofas, step 3.*

Figure 4-13 *Lounge setting, step 3.*

Tables

Figures 4-14 through 4-16 show how to draw a variety of tables constructed of different materials. The images clearly demonstrate the rendering process of tables. All the descriptions for drawing the foundation materials have been introduced in Chapter 3, so please refer to that chapter.

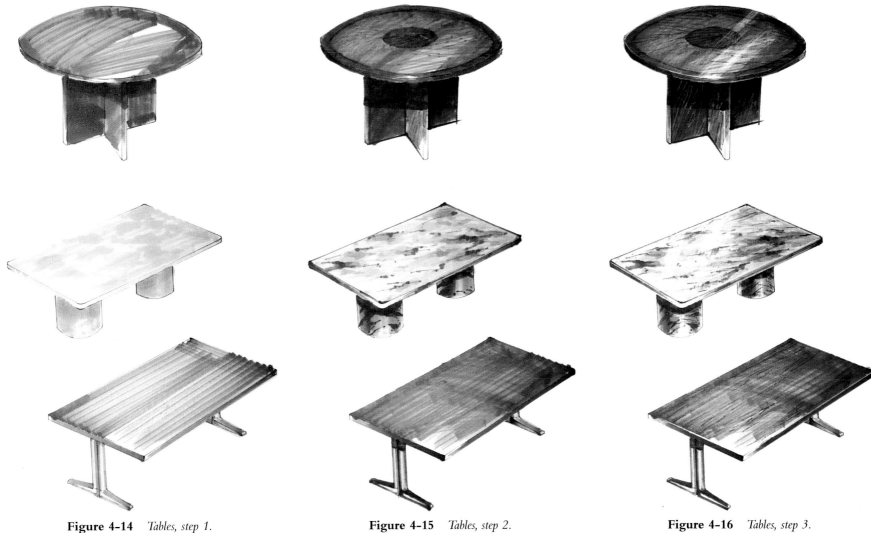

Figure 4-14 *Tables, step 1.*

Figure 4-15 *Tables, step 2.*

Figure 4-16 *Tables, step 3.*

Bookshelves

We are going to study how to render two bookshelves; one is made of wood and the other is built of metal. These two materials were discussed previously in Chapter 3 with reference to rendering metal and wood. The diagonal lines are the key to successfully rendering a metal cabinet. The clear separation between the light, dark, and shaded sides is very important for the three-dimensional effect. Always keep some light color on the lower part of the side panel of the two bookcases to represent the reflection from the floor (see Figures 4-17 through 4-19).

Figure 4-17 *Bookcases, step 1.*

Figure 4-18 *Bookcases, step 2.*

Figure 4-19 *Bookcases, step 3.*

Chests

Rendering a chest involves using lots of colored pencils to achieve the appropriate level of detail (see Figures 4–20 through 4–22).

Figure 4-20 *Chest, step 1.*

Figure 4-21 *Chest, step 2.*

Figure 4-22 *Chest, step 3.*

Office-system furniture

Figures 4-23 through 4-28 demonstrate the steps which were taken to render office-system furniture. When you render the panels of office furniture, make sure you use diagonal lines to help distinguish each separate panel even though they are the same color. When you draw the glass panel, draw everything behind the glass first, assuming there is no glass. After you finish rendering those objects inside the room, use white colored pencil to draw highlights for the glass. Use the fine tip of the pencil to draw the diagonal lines on the sharply highlighted area. With the side of the pencil, fade out some areas and make the glass realistic.

Figure 4-23   *Office-system furniture, step 1.*   **Figure 4-24**   *Office-system furniture, step 2.*

Figure 4-25   *Office-system furniture, step 3.*

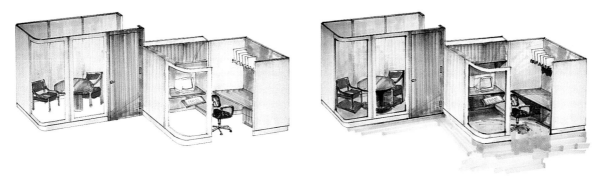

Figure 4-26 *Office-system furniture, step 4.*   **Figure 4-27** *Office-system furniture, step 5.*

Figure 4-28 *Office-system furniture, step 6.*

Other Objects Found in the Interior

Residential accessories

The following illustrations are some examples of supporting objects in the residential environment.

Kitchen appliances

Even when rendering small objects, you still need to study the three-dimensionality of each one: indicate where the light is and locate the middle and the dark sides. Then, using markers, quickly apply the basic color for each component of the objects. Use fast and slow strokes, depending on the type of surface material you are rendering. Metal and glass may need a faster stroke. Leave a spot for the highlight on the highly reflective materials such as the cover of the bread-

maker, the dishwasher, and the grill on the stove top (see Figure 4-29).

 You may use a ruler to help draw quick strokes for rapidly covering the surface.

The second step consists of drawing details for each element of an object. Make sure you clearly define the color and structure for each object. For example, the side of a breadmaker should be darker to help enhance the three-dimensionality. The shape of the control panel on the breadmaker is curved, so when it is rendered, try to make a smooth transition on this surface. Now it is time to draw the bread behind the cover of the breadmaker. Also, think about how each loaf of bread has a light and dark side. For the oven top, make sure each line on the grill has a

thickness; each should have a light side and a dark side (see Figure 4-30).

 Diagonal lines may help you to express the interreactive aspect of the environment rather than a view of all the objects in isolation. Use both the broad edge and the fine tips of markers for the creation of detail.

Finally, in the third step, use colored pencils for cleanup and to give more textures to each object. Use a sharp, white colored pencil for the edges of the microwave and grill. For the vertical edges on the appliances, push very hard from the top downward, then fade out. For horizontal edges, start at the end closest to you, making sure to get the angle of highlight on the dishwasher, microwave doors, and the cover of the breadmaker (see Figure 4-31).

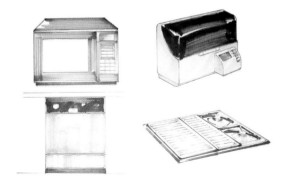

Figure 4-29 *Kitchen appliances, step 1.*

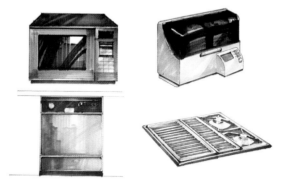

Figure 4-30 *Kitchen appliances, step 2.*

Figure 4-31 *Kitchen appliances, step 3.*

Bathroom accessories

The key to rendering bathroom accessories is the shininess. Most material in the bathroom should be highly reflective. Also, establish a good texture contrast between the sink, the counter, and the towels. The texture of the towels can be achieved by using the sides of colored pencils (see Figures 4-32 through 34).

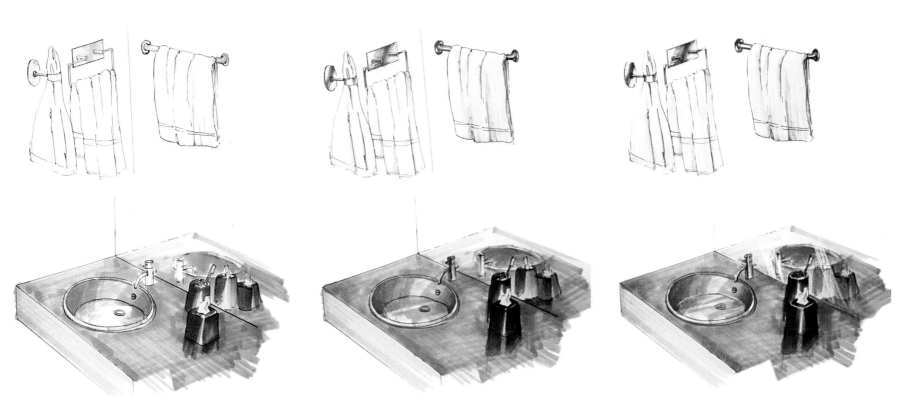

Figure 4-32 *Bathroom accessories, step 1.*   **Figure 4-33** *Bathroom accessories, step 2.*   **Figure 4-34** *Bathroom accessories, step 3.*

Curtains

Step 1: Study the folds and drape of the curtains. All curtains are composed of some flat areas and some half-cylinder shapes that represent each of the folds of the curtain. This means each fold should have a highlight area, light and dark area, shade, shadow, and reflection areas. Then note each separate curtain's pattern and texture. When you start drawing, save a highlight area, which should be vertical on the curtain's surface. Using the flat edge of a light marker, draw the light side of each curtain. This color should be very close to the base color of each curtain. Then use the flat tip of a medium-value marker to draw the dark side of the curtains. Next, using the fine tip of the dark-colored marker, draw the actual folded area. The area around the tieback is where many folded layers come together, so it should be very dark (see Figure 4-35).

> **TIP** Using the different sides of the marker will help you more effectively draw the curtains.

> **TIP** Use the middle-value marker to draw the transition from light to dark or use the same light color twice to show a value change.

Step 2: Draw the pattern on the curtains. Remember the whole shape or the geomet-

ric patterns only appear on the large flat areas of the curtains. Pattern areas that fall on the fold should only show part of the pattern. The color of the pattern on the folded area should change. For example, if the pattern is red flowers, the flowers should be light red on the light side and darker red on the folded side (see Figure 4-36).

Step 3: Add detail with a colored pencil. This will also help you add texture to the

curtains. Do not forget to darken for the shadows and make the folding areas several layers. Using the side of the colored pencil, lightly go over the entire golden-colored curtain to help unify the texture and pattern. If the curtain is transparent, now is the time to draw the frame behind it. Make the window frame behind the curtain show unevenly. Some areas should be more easily seen than others. The window frame behind the flat

Figure 4-35   *Curtains, step 1.*

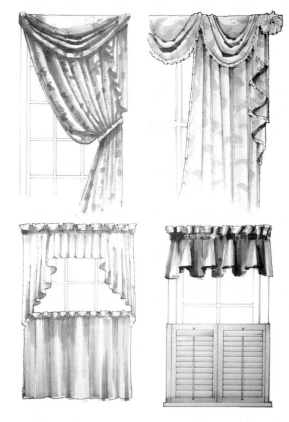

Figure 4-36   *Curtains, step 2.*

part of the curtain should be darker than behind the folding section since the folding part is more opaque (see Figure 4-37).

Step 4: Use white colored pencil to draw the highlight area on each of the folds. Push very hard on the highlight area. Then with the side of the pencil, fade the highlight out to blend in better. Once again, consider the three-dimensionality. Unify all the patterns

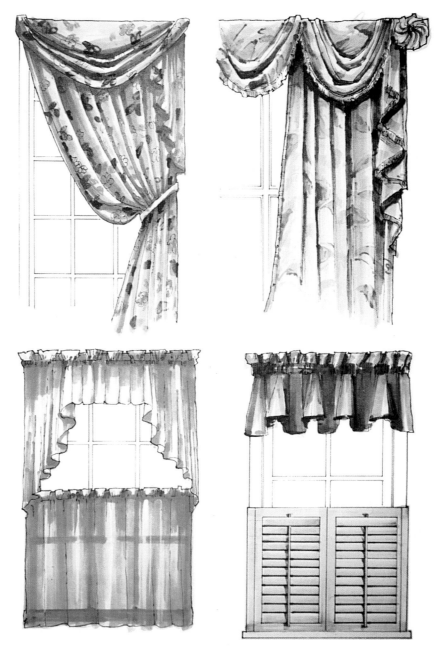

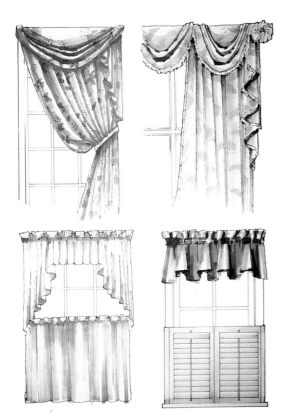

Figure 4-37 *Curtains, step 3.*

Figure 4-38 *Curtains, step 4.*

and folding areas. Put a reflection on the dark side of the fold. The reflection's color should be close to the base color of each of the curtains (see Figure 4–38).

Figures 4–39 through 4–44 provide visual resources for some other objects in interiors.

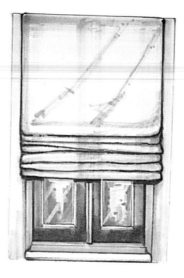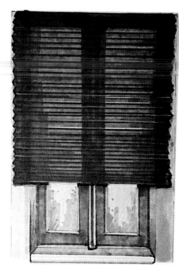

Figure 4-39   *Three window treatments.*

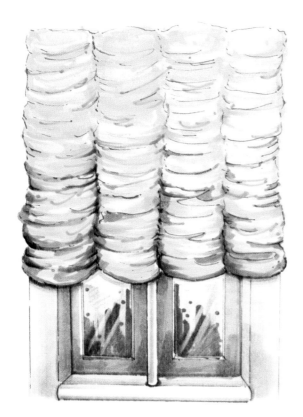

Figure 4-40   *A Roman shade window treatment.*

Figure 4-41   *Logs in a metal basket.*

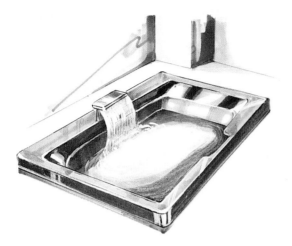

Figure 4-42 *Bathtub.*

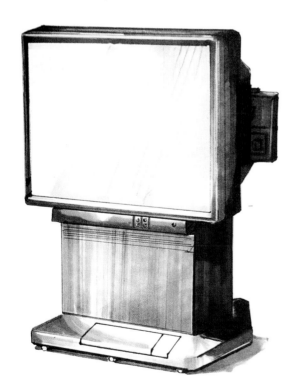

Figure 4-43 *A television set.*

Figure 4-44 *Chairs.*

Commercial environments

Office accessories and computers
The loose strokes and diagonal lines provide a smooth transition from light to dark on the computer screen and on the sides of various pieces of office equipment. It also implies the high-tech feel of the modern office accessories (see Figures 4-45 through 4-51).

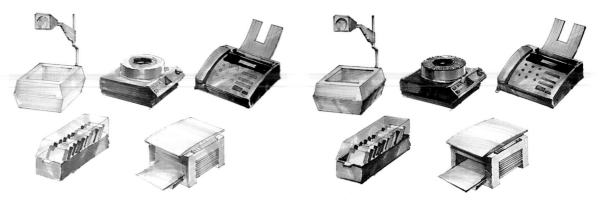

Figure 4-45   *Office equipment and accessories, step 1.*   **Figure 4-46**   *Office equipment and accessories, step 2.*

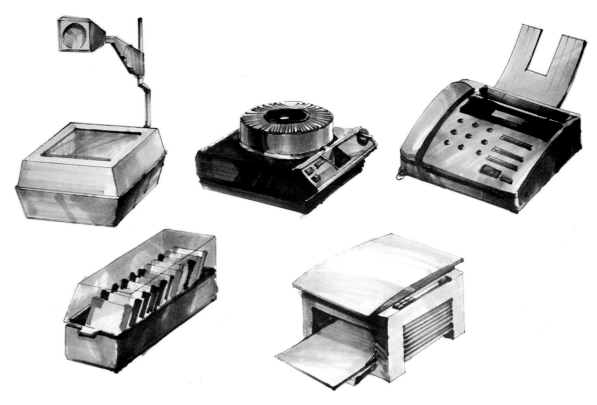

Figure 4-47   *Office equipment and accessories, step 3.*

Figure 4-48 *Computer, step 1.*

Figure 4-49 *Computer, step 2.*

Figure 4-50 *Computer, step 3.*

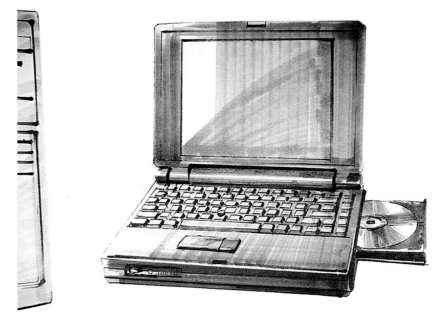

Figure 4-51 *Computer, step 4.*

Bulletin boards

Draw the basic color to construct the bulletin
board first. Then put diagonal lines on the
top to represent the glass on top of the board
(see Figures 4-52 through 4-54).

Figure 4-52   *Bulletin board, step 1.*

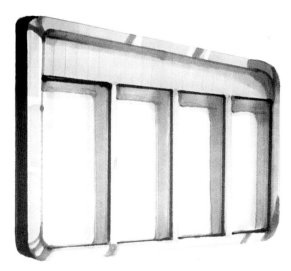

Figure 4-53   *Bulletin board, step 2.*

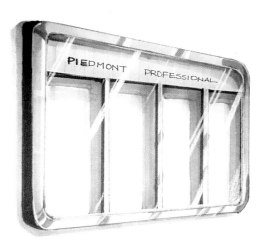

Figure 4-54   *Bulletin board, step 3.*

Exercise machines

Exercise machines are usually made of highly reflective materials, so leave a highlight and be loose when you render them (see Figures 4–55 through 4-57).

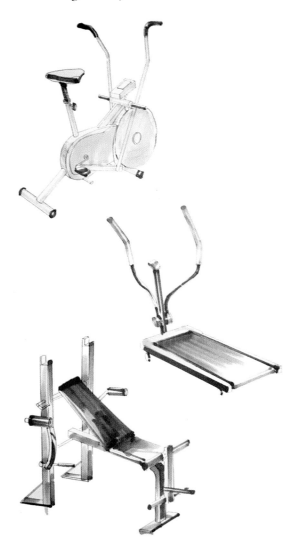

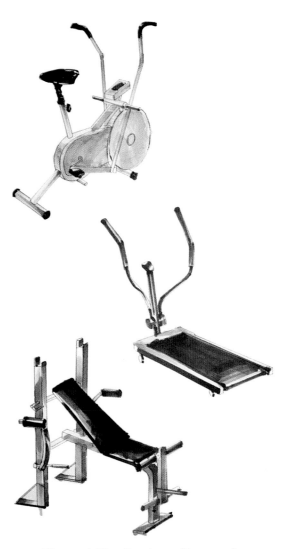

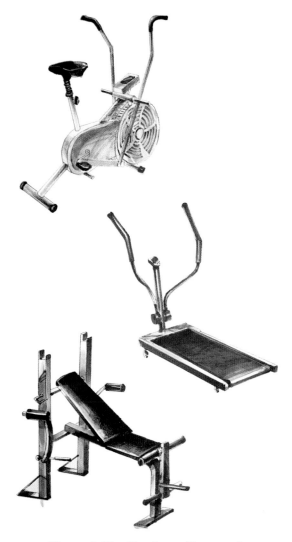

Figure 4-55 *Exercise machines, step 1.*

Figure 4-56 *Exercise machines, step 2.*

Figure 4-57 *Exercise machines, step 3.*

Display cases

In this exercise, we will render two display cases which consist of several different materials.

Step 1: Separate all different sides of the cases and decide which side is light, medium, and dark. Then, using the broad edge of the marker, very quickly begin with a basic color for each element on the two different display cases. After you decide where the highlight area on the case will be, use a light marker to draw diagonal lines from both sides of the highlight stripe. Then, draw the merchandise inside the glass cases (see Figure 4-58).

 Assume there is no glass on both cases and wait until after another step to render the glass.

Step 2: Because the glass display area hangs over the marble support base for the upright case, the glass display should make a shadow on the marble base. Use the broad edge of the marker to add more contrast between the three sides and use the fine tip of the light marker to draw the marble grain. Then layer them vertically, making sure that some of the second layer is on top of the first layer and keeping some of the first layer uncovered. The second- and the third-darker markers may be used for more intense grains. Also, you may use the point of the tip to help you enrich the marble textures. A very dark shadow on the base can help define the structure of the display case. The shadow on the light side of the marble base should be much stronger; the contrast should be more intense.

 Divide the marble into tiles. It is very helpful to identify the character of the marble.

Before you draw glass, define the merchandise inside both cases first. Give shadow, highlight, and a dark side for each piece of merchandise. When drawing the glass case on the top of the marble base, start using light gray first. Some glass pieces may be darker than others because you see through two or three panes. In this stage, for the metal support case, you can also use the second-, third-, or even fourth-darker shades of gray to give it more smooth gradation for the reflection on a metal surface (see Figure 4-59).

Step 3: To give more definition to the textures of each material, draw highlights by using several different colored pencils. With a darker-brown colored pencil, use a turn-tip technique to draw more marble grain on top of the grain that you have already drawn, but do not cover all of the marble grain you have previously drawn with markers. The light side of the base may need a darker color for grain, and the darker side of the marble support needs a light, warm color to represent reflection on the grain. Using a dark and light line technique to draw the two marble tiles closest to you, make sure the white highlight never goes across the grout. Using a white colored pencil, draw a diagonal line as a highlight on the glass and metal surfaces. The direction of the highlight on the top of the glass case should be different from the vertical panes. Draw a black, dark line under the two display cases to help clean up their shape and add three-dimensionality (see Figure 4-60).

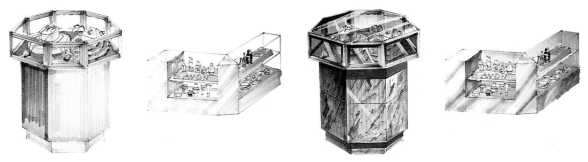

Figure 4-58 *Display cases, step 1.*   **Figure 4-59** *Display cases, step 2.*

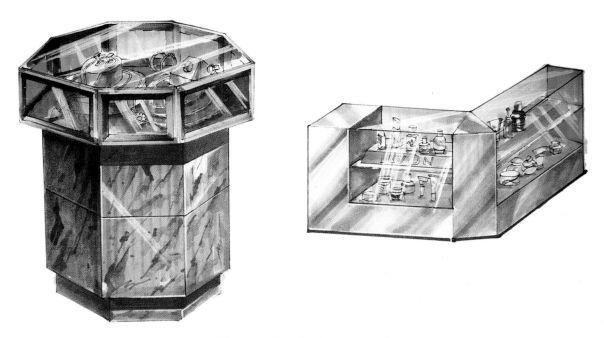

Figure 4-60 *Display cases, step 3.*

Plant and landscape elements

Water fountain

To render water, the main concern is the
nature of the water, which is transparent. So,
start by using the broad edge of the marker
to draw the basic colors and textures that
form the composition of the fountain; then
use a blue marker to render the water areas.
When you draw the water, remember that it
is moving, so it should not be flat. It should
have light, dark, and highlight areas. To
achieve this, use the blue colors in an uneven
fashion. Then use both a light-blue and a
white colored pencil to draw the highlight
on the water. If there are too many layers and
the white does not show up, then use white
paint (see Figures 4-61 through 4-63).

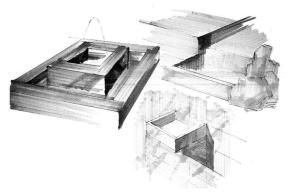

Figure 4-61   *Water fountains, step 1.*

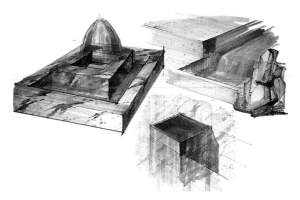

Figure 4-62   *Water fountains, step 2.*

Figure 4-63   *Water fountains, step 3.*

Green plants

Different plants have a variety of leaves, shapes, and structures. One challenge in drawing plants is to think of the whole plant as a single entity, not just separate groups of leaves. Effectively using different tips of the markers and different strokes can better represent various plants. The loose strokes and various line types and dots are the keys to successfully drawing plants.

First, abstract the basic geometrical shape of the plant. For example, in Figure 4-64, you can abstract *a* and *d* as cylinders, and *b* and *c* as a spheres. By using different colors and different types of line techniques, you can draw a base color as well as define their structure (see Figure 4-64).

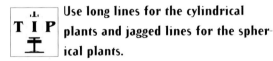

TIP Use long lines for the cylindrical plants and jagged lines for the spherical plants.

Next, use a dark green color to render each plant and enrich the layering. The emphasis should be on making the plants three-dimensional (see Figure 4-65).

Finally, use your colored pencil and fine-tip marker to define a couple of leaves on each plant. These defining lines should help to show the shape, structure, and shadows more clearly. They should also be located on the highlight area closest to you. Use light-green pencil to draw the leaves on top of the dark-green area and use a dark-green pencil to draw the leaves on the light-green side (see Figure 4-66).

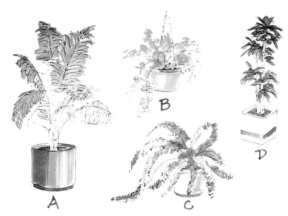

Figure 4-64 *Green plants, step 1: (a) a cylindrical plant; (b) a spherical plant; (c) a spherical plant; and (d) a cylindrical plant.*

Figure 4-65 *Green plants, step 2.*

Figure 4-66 *Green plants, step 3.*

Floral arrangements

Before you start drawing, analyze the flowers. View the flowers as a cluster and construct the bouquet as a three-dimensional shape. You can treat them as round balls or cylinders.

Step 1: Start with a light marker for each flower. Make sure you employ very loose strokes. Use different sides of the marker and different strokes for all the flowers because flowers and leaves are very individual looking. When you are working on the first colors, do not be afraid to go out of the lines. Some flowers may require the use of the flat tip, others may require the use of the fine tip—it just depends on the nature of the flowers. If the vase is transparent, go ahead and draw the stems of the flowers first. Next, put more detail on the flowers (see Figure 4-67).

Step 2: Think of the shape of the flowers and bouquet as a ball. It should have a bright side, dark side, and some reflection. The flower on the dark side of the bouquet should be darker than the others of the same color. The bouquet will make shadows on the vase, particularly directly underneath the flowers. In this step, you may use different colors or the same colors multiple times to enrich and give more depth to the flowers. Use the fine tip to define each bouquet. There should be a couple flowers on the light side and this is where they should show the

most detail and have the highest contrast (see Figure 4-68).

> **T I P** **You may also use the jagged-line technique to outline the petals and leaves. Colored pencil can enhance the outline, also. Use a light colored pencil on top of dark markers and dark colored pencil on top of light markers. Use a very dark color underneath the bouquet as a shadow.**

Step 3: Use paint or any opaque color to add more freshness to each bouquet. For example, use yellow paint to go over the yellow marker; that flower will be more pronounced. Think again about the basic principles of drawing a sphere when trying to finish a drawing. Each petal should be a little blurry on the dark side close to the edges. The flowers' petals should be very well defined in the center at the highlighted area around the whole bouquet (see Figure 4-69).

Figure 4-67   *Floral arrangement, step 1*

Figure 4-68   *Floral arrangement, step 2.*

Figure 4-69 *Floral arrangement, step 3.*

Interior architectural components

Doors

In general, when you are rendering doors or windows, leaving a door or window ajar helps to identify the objects within, giving more detail and contrast to what you see through the opening as opposed to the views you see through the glass on the door or window. The views you see through the glass should be of less contrast and a little flatter (see Figures 4-70 through 4-74).

TIP There must be shade, shadow, and highlight on the doors—they are not just one flat panel. Assume the light is coming from the top, so underneath each curved area should be a shadow.

Figure 4-70   *Doors, step 1.*

Figure 4-71   *Doors, step 2.*

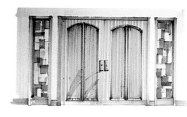

Figure 4-72   *Doors, step 3.*

Figure 4-73   *Doors, step 4.*

Figure 4-74   *Doors, step 5.*

Skylight windows

Step 1: When you draw a skylight, always start with the blue sky or the background first, assuming there is no glass in front of the skylight. When drawing the wood frame, use the marker with quick strokes to apply the basic color. Start with lots of pressure and then fade out. Leave some white space on the side of the window frame because those pieces receive direct light; it also represents the shining light (see Figure 4-75).

Step 2: Consider how to best represent the skylight. It is almost like drawing artificial light in an interior environment. In other words, there must be a dark background contrasted with the bright lights, so the ceiling inside should be dark (see Figure 4-76).

TIP The elements closest to you should have stronger contrasts than the others. You should use a ruler and the fine tip of the marker for fine details.

Step 3: Draw more detail on the window opening areas. For example, draw more detail on the trees by using the layering technique to make them more three-dimensional. Make the trees, which show through the glass, a little faded. Using your white colored pencil, draw diagonal lines to show the glass. Clean up your lines on the window frames (see Figure 4-77).

Figure 4-75 *Skylight windows, step 1.*

Figure 4-76 *Skylight windows, step 2.*

Figure 4-77 *Skylight windows, step 3.*

Stairs

In general, when drawing stairs, the biggest concern will be how to best represent the structural elements. Defining the light source always helps in drawing interior architectural elements such as stairs. Typically, the top of steps are lighter, and a highlight always appears on the edges of steps (see Figures 4-78 to 4-80).

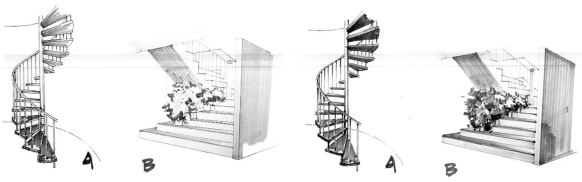

Figure 4-78   *Stairs, step 1.*

Figure 4-79   *Stairs, step 2.*

Figure 4-80   *Stairs, step 3.*

Columns

Analyze the structure and character of each column. Start drawing the shade and shadow. Then create value changes on the columns (see Figure 4-81).

After you have given the object a base color, then you refine it by giving more contrast to the geometric shapes, adding more texture, and blending the gradation of light to dark so there is not such a great contrast on the column. Use both tips of the marker and also both sides of the pencil (see Figure 4-82).

Use colored pencil to clean up and emphasize the major structure. For example, because a column is cylindrical in shape, there must be reflection and highlights to make the column look realistic (see Figure 4-83).

 Remember all reflection and highlights on columns should be vertically oriented.

 Use a warm, bright color for reflection on the far edge of the dark side because, generally, interiors have warm color sources.

Figure 4-81 *Columns, step 1.*

Figure 4-82 *Columns, step 2.*

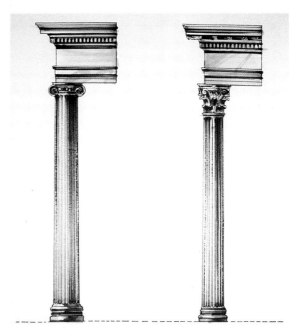

Figure 4-83 *Columns, step 3.*

Fireplace

To draw a fireplace composed of rock, abstract the shape of the fireplace as a three-dimensional block. The top will probably receive the most light; the front face would receive secondary light; and the side of the fireplace would probably be the darkest. When you start, separate all sides or faces of the fireplace and do the basic color with the broad edge of a marker. The firebox in the center of the fireplace, where there is no light, should be very dark (see Figure 4-84).

TIP Even in this first stage, you should be thinking about a reflection on the shiny surfaces. Regardless of the basic material of the fireplace, the color on the wall should be dark as should the reflection on the floor.

Step 2: Now, work on reproducing the textures of the materials. For a stone fireplace, use two or three gray colors to render the different pieces of rocks. Using the darker fine-tip markers, fill in the mortared joints and clean up each piece. Be sure to use different techniques for different materials. For example, we already started using short, flat lines for rocks, just dots for granite texture, the turn-tip technique for marble, and diagonal lines for metal. Another objective at this stage is to enhance the three-dimensionality

by clarifying the structure of each of the fireplaces (see Figure 4-85).

Step 3: This is a very detailed stage in finishing all fireplaces. To finish the stone fireplace, use different colored markers and colored pencils, but in the same tone, for various pieces of stone. You may even try the same marker or colored pencil, applying different pressures on the pieces and sections of stone to create multiple layers. Also, you may use the side of a colored pencil to render the textures of the stones. On the light side of the stone, there should be more noticeable textures than on the dark side.

To finish the granite fireplace, use the fine tip of a light marker, then make dots or stipple the area with a darker marker. Eventually, stipple the granite with a colored pencil to enhance the texture of the granite. In defining the reflection on the floor for the image on the lower right, use the same color and same texture of the fireplace by extending the vertical line on the wall straight down. The reflection should have less contrast than the actual fireplace. Then use white or a light colored pencil to draw diagonal lines as a reflection. Continue those diagonal lines across the reflections on the floor to unify the floor as one flat surface. Make sure the firebox is dark, without reflections or any other value changes. The firebox should make a good contrast with the surface of the fireplace (see Figure 4-86).

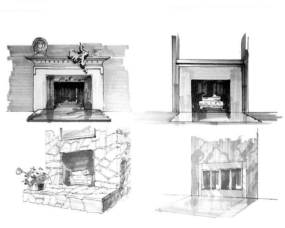

Figure 4-84 *Fireplace, step 1.*

Figure 4-85 *Fireplace, step 2.*

Figure 4–86 *Fireplace, step 3.*

Wood panel

In design, walls and panels are not always flat. Rendering a section of a panel is a good way to study how light affects shading and the way shadows fall. Before you start rendering, study the section of the panel to gain a better understanding of the variations of the surface.

First, you should very carefully study how the section correlates to the elevation. If the light is coming from a 45-degree angle on the left side, then the continuous dadoed area (which is shown by the numbered areas 1 and 9 in Figure 4-87) will be completely shadowed. Areas 1 and 9 should be the darkest of the entire drawing. Area 2 will probably be a little lighter because it stands up higher. It should be a medium lightness. Area 3 faces the light; this means it directly receives light, so it should be very bright. Area 4 is the highest point on the entire panel, so it should receive the most light. It will be the point of highest contrast in the drawing. Area 5 is against the light because of the slope of the panel, so it should be dark. The lower part of the area should reflect some light from area 6, so the top part of area 5 should be darker than the lower part. Area 6 is also almost totally facing the light, but not quite as directly as area 3, so it should not be as light as area 3 but lighter than the flat part of area 2. Area 7 should be treated the same as area 2. Area 8 should have a shadow because area 7 is raised up from the flat panel of area 8, and

it will make a shadow there; area 8 should be dark. Area 9 should be treated the same as area 1 because no light can penetrate. Area 10 is the normal color area. the neutral color of the panel since there is not much light interaction; there are four of these areas.

Now select four different values of colors for the wood from light, medium, and dark shades. Use the flat edge of the light-colored marker to very quickly define the three-dimensional structure and show where there

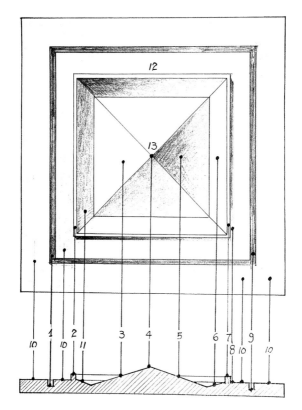

Figure 4-87   *Wood panel, step 1.*

are lighter and darker areas. Use the dark marker to very quickly shade in area 1 since that area is definitely the darkest area. Using the same marker, draw in area 8 as a shadow. Make sure that the shadow for area 8 only appears on the right and bottom sides of the drawing. Using the second-darkest marker, draw the sides against the light such as in areas 5, 11, 12 and 13. Now use the light color to draw all the area 10s. Make sure you leave some white space in some areas, such as area 3. This is the area with the highest contrast. The lightest corner should be treated as the second-highest contrast area because it is close to the light source (see Figure 4-88).

To begin the detailing and refining, think about how to separate all the different pieces on the same panel. Keep in mind that all the panels are different; they are not just one flat piece, so use strokes in different directions to help separate the various panels. After the initial step using the flat edge of the marker,

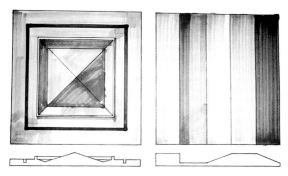

Figure 4-88   *Wood panel, step 2.*

begin using the fine tip of the marker and the turn-tip technique to draw the texture. When you draw the wood grains, make sure they go in different directions on each separate panel. It is very important to understand that they are not one flat piece but many flat pieces facing separate directions; the movement of your stroke for the grains should be different.

 Clean your ruler and marker tips every now and then.

The color of the wood grain is usually a little bit darker than the basic wood color. What you need to understand from this stage is how to use different techniques to make distinctions between the different panels at different elevations and then increase the three-dimensionality of the drawing (see Figure 4-89).

Step 3: Start using colored pencil to give more texture and contrast to the wood. When you use colored pencil, you can use both the point and the side of the lead to give it texture. Make sure you are using the turn-tip technique for the wood grains. For area 5, you may start using very dark color on the corner of the triangular-shaped area and gradually lighten up as you go toward the bottom of this area. Use the colored pencil to go over the grain that you already drew with the marker. When using colored pencil

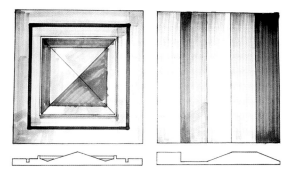

Figure 4-89   *Wood panel, step 3.*

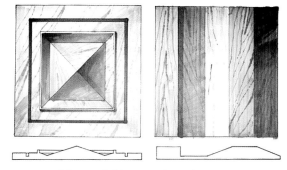

Figure 4-90   *Wood panel, step 4.*

Figure 4-91   *Wood panel, step 5.*

make sure to apply different amounts of pressure (see Figure 4-90).

Step 4: Think about the reflections and the highlights. All the edges on the panels should receive the light, so you should be using a ruler and a white colored pencil and the lift-stroke technique to draw the highlight. Also since area 3 receives most of the light, you should be using the side of the colored pencil. Start at the top with lots of pressure, then fade out as you go to the bottom, decreasing the amount of pressure. The bottom of area 5 should have reflections from area 6. Since area 6 is a warm color, the reflection should be a warm color. The reflection should only go on the bottom half of area 5. Use a white colored pencil or a light color to clean up the edges of the drawing because sometimes markers bleed out of the lines you first drew (see Figure 4-91).

Lighting fixtures

Table lamps

First, analyze the characteristics of each lamp. What are the basic geometric shapes that compose each lamp? What are the materials of each component? How do the light rays travel from the light source? Then use the broad edge of the markers from light to dark to give a base color and three-dimensionality to the object. After some detailed steps, use a bright, light colored pencil to draw the light rays (see Figures 4-92 through 4-94).

Figure 4-93   *Table lamps, step 2.*

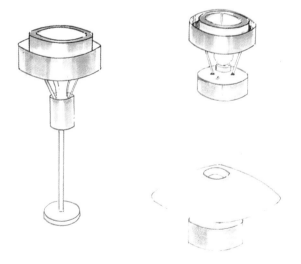

Figure 4-92   *Table lamps, step 1.*

Figure 4-94   *Table lamps, step 3.*

Chandelier

The key to success is to treat the light fixture as a whole object, not just individual parts, such as the arms, stem, and glass shades.

Step 1: Start by abstracting the basic geometrical shape of the chandelier. Then give a base color to each of the components. Treat them all as three-dimensional objects. Each arm and stem should have dark, light, highlight, and reflection areas (see Figure 4-95).

Step 2: Use several dark colors to give more three-dimensionality to all the parts of the chandelier. Emphasize the basic structure of each component of the chandelier (see Figure 4-96).

Step 3: Unify the entire structure into a single object. Use colored pencil and marker to draw many details on the arms and glass shades nearest you. If necessary use the broad edge of the light marker or the side of the colored pencil to reduce the contrast on the glass shades on the back of the chandelier. This will help give the object have more depth (see Figure 4-97).

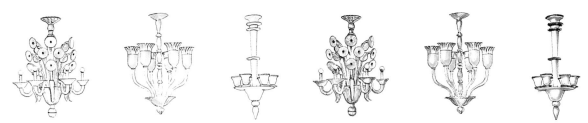

Figure 4-95 *Chandeliers, step 1.*   **Figure 4-96** *Chandeliers, step 2.*

Figure 4-97 *Chandeliers, step 3.*

Using colored paper to draw light fixtures
As we mentioned before, colored paper provides uniform tones for the rendering. Medium values of colored paper can be most effective in representing a highlight or any light-dominated drawing.

Step 1: Use a light-colored marker to apply a basic color for each fixture. Leave the reflection and highlight areas open (see Figure 4-98).

Step 2: Add darkness for depth and use marker to refine the structure and the thickness of each element. Make a smooth transition from the dark areas to the highlight areas (see Figure 4-99).

Step 3: Use colored pencil to draw the highlight and the light rays. In most light areas, the highlight should be drawn, using the tip of your white pencil. The rays on the walls or objects should be done using the side of the pencil to fade out from the strongest light area (see Figure 4-100).

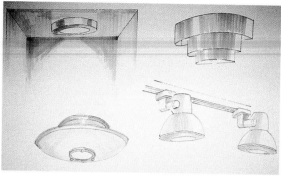

Figure 4-98   *Light fixtures with colored paper, step 1.*

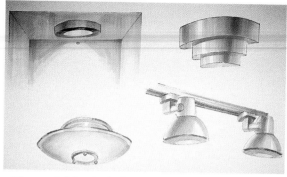

Figure 4-99   *Light fixtures with colored paper, step 2.*

Figure 4-100   *Light fixtures with colored paper, step 3.*

People

First, you need to visually abstract the human body to its basic geometric shapes. For example, the trunk of the body could be considered a rectangle and the head a sphere. On the other hand, remember that the human body cannot be completely reduced to geometric shapes, it has its own peculiar anomalies.

Start by using the broad edge of the marker with different quick strokes to follow the movement of the body to provide the light and dark separation for each of the figures. Make sure to leave white space for the highlight area (see Figure 4-101). The second layer of color should be the primary color of the object. In this case it is the color of the figure's clothing. Also, the second color is the color used to make the transition from dark to the highlight (see Figure 4-102).

Next, start thinking about the textures of the clothing and then use colored pencil and the fine tip of the marker to add more darkness in the shaded areas (see Figures 4-103 and 4-104)

TIP Think about where your light source is located. This will always help you define the three-dimensionality.

Figure 4-101   *People, step 1.*

Figure 4-102   *People, step 2.*

Figure 4-103   *People, step 3.*

Figure 4-104   *People, step 4.*

Chapter 5

Rendering Various Types of Interiors and Exteriors

This chapter demonstrates how to integrate the rendering of materials, finishes, and objects explained in the preceding chapter and apply the techniques to various types of interior spaces. The rendering techniques, demonstrated in previous chapters, should also be applied when you create the drawing. The effectiveness of lighting in a space should be the focus of study for most of the drawings in this chapter.

Two-Dimensional Plans and Elevations

When you render two-dimensional drawings, such as a floor plan and elevation, the highlighting and shadowing of three-dimensional objects are important factors for success. Begin with defining the light source. In Figure 5-1, the light is coming from the left side of the windows. Use the broad edge of the marker and quick strokes to provide the basic color for all elements in the plans (see Figure 5-1).

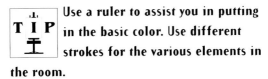 **Use a ruler to assist you in putting in the basic color. Use different strokes for the various elements in the room.**

The second stage is to add the detailing. You may want to increase the darkness on the plants, the book shelves, and on the shaded side of the sofa. Be sure to leave some white for the highlight. Also, think about the shadows; for example, the back and the arm of the sofa should be making a shadow on the seat, and the whole sofa should be making a shadow on the floor. Be sure the plants look like three-dimensional plants even in a two-dimensional drawing. They should have dark, light, highlight, and shadow areas (see Figure 5-2).

Finally, use colored pencil and the fine tip of the marker for more refining. For the plants, use ink pen and colored pencil to more clearly show detail of several leaves. Employ colored pencil to show carpet texture. Use the pencil tip to draw the pattern and the side of the pencil to draw the texture. Keep in mind that the area close to the light source (the window) should have strong contrast. Always remember to have shadow on the elevation if there is an object in front of the wall (see Figure 5-3).

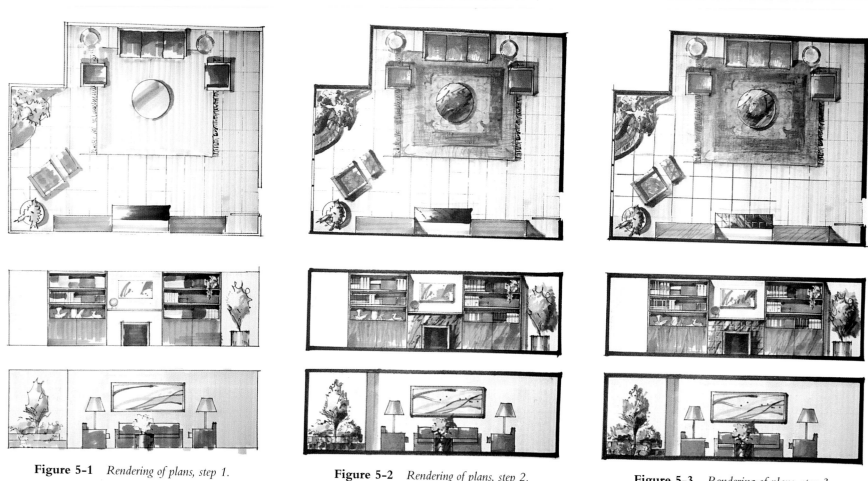

Figure 5-1 *Rendering of plans, step 1.*

Figure 5-2 *Rendering of plans, step 2.*

Figure 5-3 *Rendering of plans, step 3.*

The Effects of Lighting on Materials in Interior Spaces

Lighting changes the appearance of materials and creates a certain atmosphere. It is the element that binds all interior elements together. It can provide warm natural images for our environment; it suggests, at times, delightful, playful moods or moments of somber, subdued moods. When rendering lighting, think about how the light acts in the space and how it reflects on other materials.

Daylight

In this exercise the materials involved are glass, carpet, wood, and marble. The featured lighting will be artificial and natural.

Begin by creating the impression and feeling of the space first. Apply the basic color of each element within the space, dividing the shade and shadow areas on the floor. Use the lift-stroke technique for the shadow of the window divider on the floor (see Figure 5-4).

Then, study more of the space. Decide where the most highly contrasted area should be. There are several areas that should be high in contrast. The corner of the desk, which is close to the window, should have the most contrast. When you render, you should leave some highlight on the top of the

desk to reflect the light from the coving light. The shadow on the side of the desk should be much stronger, then, because it is also much closer to the light source from the window. The second high-contrast area is the shadow on the back wall and on the floor. The contrast is reduced as you move away from the window toward the right side of the desk. Use this concept to draw the floor and wall shadows (see Figure 5-5).

To draw the coving light, shade the ceiling first to provide the dark background and show the contrast of the light. The left wood panel in front of the cove light, which is totally against the direction of the incoming daylight, should be the darkest. The light behind the center panel on the coving light should be bright and then grow darker toward the center of the ceiling. The panel facing the windows should be lighter because it receives some daylight.

 By using diagonal lines, you can improve the reflections and the transition from dark to light.

Also, at this stage, draw the landscape forms, which should appear on the outside of the window. Assume there is no glass on the window yet. Think about elements of the landscape, such as plants, land, clouds, and mountains, which should be three-

dimensional, with a dark, light, and shadow side (see Figure 5-5).

The next step should focus on refining and giving the feeling of distance to the space. First, refine, using colored pencils to clean up the object's edges. When you use markers in the first and second steps, they may go out of the lines. The colored pencils are used to clean them up. Use darker colored pencils for very high-contrast areas, such as the first corner of the desk, the front or first shadow of the window frame, and the corner of the back wall, and the ceiling which casts a shadow.

Use colored pencil to create more detailed wood grain, and use the side of the colored pencil to give texture to the carpeting.

Next, use white colored pencil to draw a vertical line for the curved part of the glass and a diagonal line as a highlight for the flat part of the glass window. Also, use the straight point of the light colored pencil to draw quick lines on the edges of the desk to separate the different sides.

From now on, we move from concentrating on rendering single or individual objects to creating a sense of space, which changes with distance. The most common ways to achieve this change is to give stronger contrasts to the objects close to you. The color should be brighter on the objects or elements close to you than on those further away (see Figure 5-6).

Figure 5-4   *Rendering of daylight, step 1.*

Figure 5-5   *Rendering of daylight, step 2.*

Figure 5-6   *Rendering of daylight, step 3.*

Recessed lights

When rendering a space which has artificial light as the primary light source, the higher contrast and the perceived change in distance always help to communicate your design. So, when you apply the basic color on all the elements in the room, leave the white area on top of the desk and the corner on the face of the marble wall as a high-reflection area.

Also, at this point, consider the reflection on the shiny floor. To create the reflection, apply the basic color that was used on the vertical objects in the room to the floor. First, use light blue, which was also used for the basic tone of the reflection of the marble desk on the floor. Use light, warm gray to extend the color of the glass block onto the floor.

The ceiling should be dark at the back and have a little bit of light in front. When you render the recessed light fixtures, consider their cylindrical shape. They should have a highlight, a light side, and a dark side. Also,

keep in mind we are rendering a space that has depth, so the three recessed lights in the front row should have higher contrast than the three in the back rows (see Figure 5-7).

The first corner of the marble desk should have the strongest shadow along with the corner of the vertical marble wall because those corners are closest to the light sources as well as to you. The reflection on the floor should be thought of as a mirror image, so the direction of the grain should be opposite of the actual object. The glass blocks should have a variety of colors with the same tone on the different pieces. Using short strokes for the glass blocks, draw each block with different pressures (see Figure 5-8).

The next step is to draw more detail in the materials with an emphasis on creating a sense of depth in the space. The pieces of glass block that are closest to you should have the most detail. To draw details, use colored pencil to apply textures and ink pen to separate each piece. Make sure the same high contrast of glass block is reflected on the floor, too.

For the marble desk, divide the marble into tiles to give a clearer definition of the material. Use dark-blue colored pencil for grain. The light side of the marble should have a medium-colored grain; the dark side should have the darkest grain. For the reflection area on the dark side, the grain should be lighter.

For the recessed lights, use a very sharp white colored pencil to draw the light rays on both sides of the light source. Then, using the flat side of the pencil, fade out from the center of the light and move down.

To render the floor, in order to define the tiles, use ink lines to go over all the reflections. Then, using white colored pencil, draw the highlight on the side edge of each tile.

Make sure you define only in the selected areas—not every single piece. The most important thing is to represent depth in the room. This is partially done by paying attention to the objects closest to you, which should have higher contrast and clearer textures. Objects farther away should be faded (see Figure 5-9).

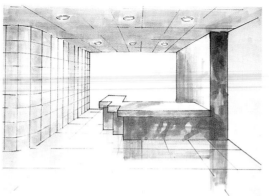

Figure 5-7   *Rendering of recessed light, step 1.*   **Figure 5-8**   *Rendering of recessed light, step 2.*

Figure 5-9   *Rendering of recessed light, step 3.*

Reflected lighting

In this exercise, the materials involved are brick, wood paneling, and carpet.

Step 1: Quickly apply the basic color with a very strong sense of three-dimensional separation for all elements within the space. Always save an area on each surface for reflections from the lighting source. In Figure 5-10, the area of reflection is the top of the desk and some area on the wall. Use a ruler to help you draw each piece of brick (see Figure 5-10).

Step 2: Analyze the space one step further before you draw more details. The bottom of the light fixtures do not receive any light, so they should be very dark. This can provide good background contrast with the lighting. The one lighting tube closest to you should be the darkest one among the four tubes. To render the brick wall, because each brick is different from the next, try using markers with different pressures to draw the different sizes of the bricks in the wall. Use colored pencil or the fine tip of the marker to draw several bricks that are close to you or close to the light source. When you draw the ceiling, the areas close to the wall as well as the center of the ceiling should be darker. Areas closest to the light fixtures should be bright (see Figure 5-11).

Step 3: Start on the wood panels by applying a basic wood color first. Also, start to draw a pattern on the floor. Then, use colored pencil to clean up the lines and make sure the highest-contrast areas are closest to you. Use the side of the colored pencil to give texture to the wall, carpet, and a little on the brick. Use a sharp, white colored pencil again to draw the edge of the light fixtures to help heighten the contrast, particularly for the tube closest to you (see Figure 5-12).

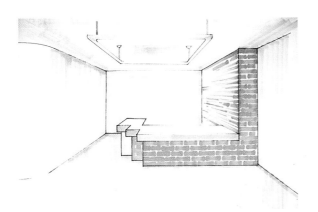

Figure 5-10 *Reflected track light, step 1.*

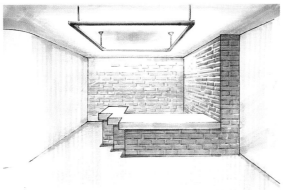

Figure 5-11 *Reflected track light, step 2.*

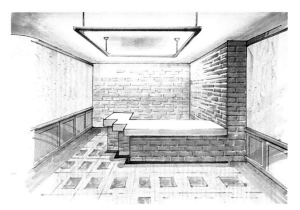

Figure 5-12 *Reflected track light, step 3.*

Evening

Step 1: Apply a basic color to all the materials while keeping in mind the need to separate the light and dark sides on the desk, ceiling panels, and window dividers. Use the broad edge of the markers to draw straight lines up and down for the walls and the floors. Using a diagonal line for the metals.

Because it is nighttime and objects outside the window are unclear, the landscape elements should be almost two-dimensional. Therefore, use two or three darker-gray colors to draw the scene outside the windows (see Figure 5-13).

Step 2: Do more refining for each of the materials. The diagonal line on the metal desk should be reflected into the mirror wall. As it is reflected in the mirror, the direction of the diagonal line should be reversed. To draw the ceiling metal panel, put a couple freehand diagonal lines in the center of the ceiling panel by the cove light to help give it a more integrated feeling. Be sure that the two corners of the cove light closest to you have much stronger contrast than the two corners closest to the back wall (see Figure 5-14).

Step 3: Use colored pencil and some fine-tip markers to refine some more. More dark shading on the ceiling is needed as contrast to help show the cove light.

Draw the windows, make the glass dark blue, and apply some blue color on the window frames to represent the evening blue colors shining on the frame. Using sharp diagonal lines helps to show the reflections on the mirrors and windows. Vertical highlights should be added on the curve of the window. Press hard at the top and then lighter at the bottom since the upper highlight of the glass is closer to the light source (see Figure 5-15).

TIP You may divide the metal by tile, using the dark and light line technique to draw detail on the pieces closest to you. The pink color of the floor should be reflected into the metal and the frame of the windows.

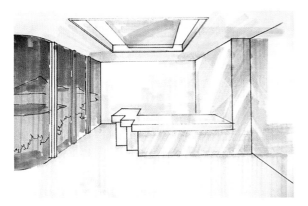

Figure 5-13 *Evening scene, step 1.*

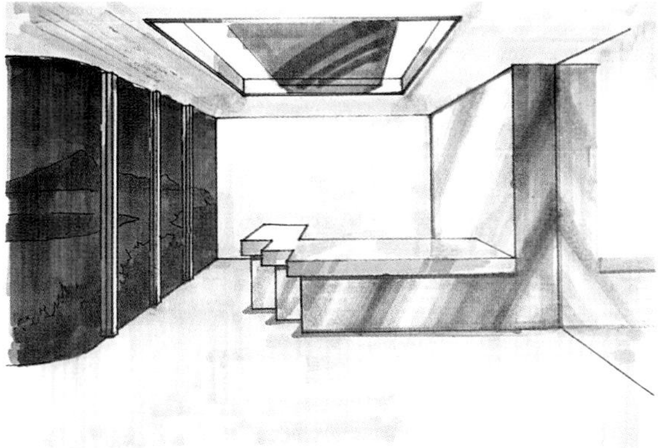

Figure 5-14 *Evening scene, step 2.*

Figure 5-15 *Evening scene, step 3.*

Evening scenes with colored paper

Colored paper can be very effective in rendering lighting and evening scenes. Use a medium-blue colored paper for the background, which can easily provide the overall tone for your rendering. This method can save you a lot of time because you do not have to cover the entire space with many layers of color.

Step 1: Define each light source and think about what effect it will have on the walls and other surfaces in the rendering (see Figure 5-16). Then, use markers to draw the darker values on each element to separate each side of the desk and also the wall unit. You may use the darker blue marker and a ruler to cover the floors and walls with vertical lines. You may also turn the paper upside down to draw the back wall because you are

using the lift-line technique and to save some blue paper for the light area on the back wall. So, when you start the line at the seam between the floor and wall, it will be darker and then fade out as you get to the top of the wall where the lights are.

Step 2: You want to start increasing the contrast of the light sources in all the areas. For example, you should use the dark-blue marker on both sides of the light rays coming from the lights on the left wall, then fade them out to the top of the wall. Now, enhance the darkness of the sides of the desk. Start drawing the three-dimensionality of the recessed light (see Figure 5-17).

Remember that the two lights in the front row should have a higher contrast than the two in the back row. This means the darks should be darker in the

front row than in the back row. Also, you can use the fine tip of the marker to add some detail to the shadow on the floor or the shadow on the wall.

Step 3: Using a sharp light-colored pencil, draw a very hard line around both sides of the light rays to represent their edges. Use a ruler for these two lines. Using the side of the colored pencil, shade in between the two white lines that you just drew. Make sure that the color is brighter as you get closer to the light source, then fade the colors out. Do the same thing for the recessed lights. The light has an effect on the ceiling that needs to be shown.

Make sure you use the near-color technique for drawing reflected colors on the desk. Use the sharp light colors for drawing the highlight on the edges of the desk. Also

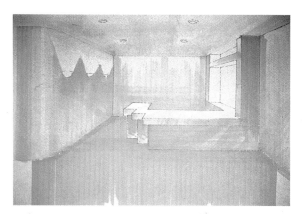

Figure 5-16   *Evening scene with colored paper, step 1.*

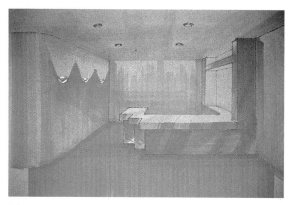

Figure 5-17   *Evening scene with colored paper, step 2.*

Figure 5-18   *Evening scene with colored paper, step 3.*

use the side of the colored pencil to add some texture to the floor, particularly in the high-contrast area, which is near the corner of the desk (see Figure 5-18).

Step 4: Draw the neon lights, using the French curve. With sharper, bright colored pencils, draw the neon tube, and then use the side of the pencils to fade them out from the curve lines (see Figure 5-19).

Figure 5-19 *Evening scene with colored paper, step 4.*

Various Types of Interior Environments

In general, before you start rendering, analyze or visualize the space you have just designed. Where is the light coming from? Which parts will be light, which parts will be dark, and where will the shadows be? How is the space structured? What materials are in the space? What technique would best help you accomplish your rendering?

Living room with fireplace

Step 1: Use the broad edge of the marker to define the structure of the room. In this stage, draw quickly (see Figure 5-20).

TIP Use a ruler to help draw the vertical wall, floors, and beams. Use short strokes of different lengths to draw the pieces of stone on the face of the fireplace. Use lines or dots to draw the basic shape of the plants.

Step 2: Start refining. Make clearer separations between the back of the sofa and the seat by adding more blue color on the back and side of the sofa. To draw the fireplace, use different colors, but limit the colors to neutral tones for the different pieces of stone on the face of the fireplace. Keep in mind the

high-contrast area should be close to the light source, which is behind the beam. This means upper-level stones will show stronger contrast than the lower pieces. In this stage, you should still be emphasizing individual objects and how to make them look three-dimensional (see Figure 5-21).

Figure 5-20   *Living room with fireplace, step 1.*

Step 3: Continue to refine and unify. The pieces of stone should each have some dark color on the right and bottom sides since the light source is coming from above and to the left. Not every single piece needs lots of detail, just the ones that are closest to you. After you finish the detail of the pieces of stone, use white colored pencil leading down

Figure 5-21   *Living room with fireplace, step 2.*

from the very top of the fireplace, then fade out to represent the reflection of the light.

Use the near-color technique to draw the interrelationship of all the colors. For example, there should be some red-orange on the couch and on top of the coffee table because of the reflection from the fireplace. The floor tile should also reflect the vertical material.

Use a diagonal line to unify the floor. Draw some of the tiles in detail that are close to you. Make sure that the light or dark lines never cross the grout (see Figure 5-22).

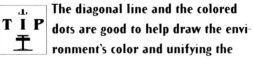 **The diagonal line and the colored dots are good to help draw the environment's color and unifying the whole tone of the space.**

Children's environment

When you render a child's environment, keep in mind that the color and the style of your rendering should capture the liveliness and innocence of childhood. The color should be bright and fresh, and the style should be free-flowing. Start with a fundamental color and give basic three-dimensionality to all the elements. After defining the details, draw diagonal lines and dots; then use near-color techniques to enhance the relationship of the fresh colors (see Figures 5-23 through 5-25).

Figure 5-23   *Children's environments, step 1.*

Figure 5-24   *Children's environments, step 2.*

Figure 5-25   *Children's environments, step 3.*

Figure 5-22   *Living room with fireplace, step 3.*

Bright-colored and highly reflective environments

When you draw an environment with several bright colors (Figure 5-26*a*), concentrate more on the interaction of the colors, expanding more on the concept of the near-color technique to enhance the reflection of each color.

 TIP **Diagonal lines, dots, and colored pencils are good for the near-color technique.**

In Figure 5-26*b*, several highly reflective materials are involved, including tiles, metal, and mirrors. You should concentrate on effectively using reflection and highlight. Start by analyzing the space you will be drawing. If the object is attached to the mir-

ror, you can extend the outline of the object into the mirror, but the lines in the mirror should not be stronger or darker than the actual object outline. The same principle applies to the color and the contrast. This means the color reflected inside the mirror should not be as strong as the color of the object in the actual space.

Start by giving a base color to the elements of the space to clearly identify what is the actual object and what is reflected in the mirror (see Figure 5-27).

The second step is to render strong contrast and reflection for all elements inside the two spaces. In Figure 5-28*b*, the mirror wall should be reflected onto the tile on the floor, and the ceiling should be extending into the mirror. When you draw the mirror, draw everything that is reflected in that mirror

first. For example, the red panel, the gray ceiling, and the light rays should be reflected in the mirror. The floor should also be reflected onto the lower part of the mirror wall (see Figure 5-28).

The next step is to clarify. After you draw multiple reflections, the surfaces of the mirror and floor do not seem to be flat any more. Using diagonal lines and the fade-out technique can be very helpful in fixing this problem by unifying the surfaces. Diagonal lines on the mirror should keep the same direction, which indicates that there is a flat surface. The direction of the diagonal lines on the floor and wall should be different. Use colored pencil to make the individual objects more refined so that you can tell the difference between the objects and their reflection in the mirror (see Figure 5-26).

Figure 5-26 *Bright-colored environments, step 3: (a) emphasizing the near-color technique; (b) emphasizing reflection and highlight.*

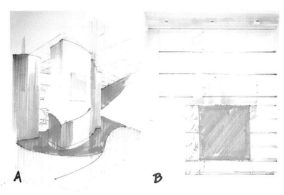

Figure 5-27 *Bright-colored environments, step 1.*

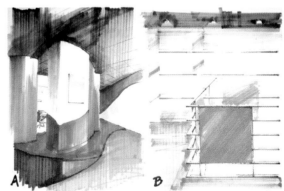

Figure 5-28 *Bright-colored environments, step 2.*

Storefront and retail displays

One of the important keys to successfully draw a retail environment is to carefully render the lighting's effect on the space. Strong contrast and bright color always help. Leave enough white space to indicate which surfaces receive direct light, then increase the darkness on the shadow areas (see Figures 5-29 through 5-31).

Figure 5-29   *Storefront and retail displays, step 1.*

Figure 5-30   *Storefront and retail displays, step 2.*

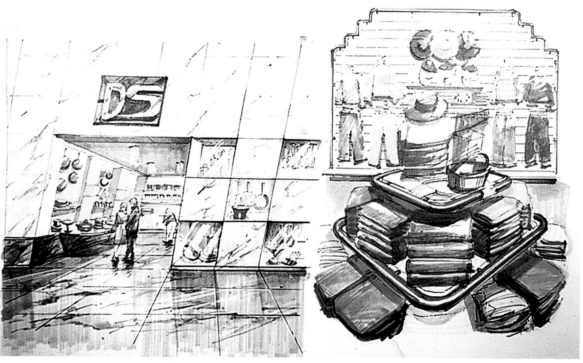

Figure 5-31   *Storefront and retail displays, step 3.*

Nightclubs

Before you draw, think about what kind of feeling you get when you walk into very active bars. The rendering of a nightclub should be vibrant with kinetic energy, in contrast to the formal living room which is often meant to be static and therefore soothing. Most bars have direct and indirect light. In addition, the colors and tones tend to be purple or bluish and a little dark. People are moving and talking, even playing. There is lots of motion involved.

Step 1: Do not render the basic color, as usual, for individual elements or objects. Instead, express a sense of motion by drawing the interaction of color in the space first (see Figure 5-32).

Step 2: This step is based on the first interaction. Render a little more intensely the basic color of each element, such as ceiling, walls, and people. For example, maybe use more blues near the ceiling and more purple near the mirrors and the floors (see Figure 5-33).

Step 3: Start refining all the elements. When you draw the people, you do not have to be very detailed. Just separate the light and dark sides on their clothing. Leave some background color on the top of the people's heads and shoulders to reaffirm the highlight (see Figure 5-34).

Step 4: Use colored pencil as the main vehicle for refining, giving a shininess and highlight to the materials (columns, mirrors, and light rays all should have really strong contrast). If the colored pencil is no longer successful because there are too many layers of mediums, you can use white paint to draw some really strong highlights, such as the light rays on the ceiling fixtures (see Figure 5-35).

Figure 5-32   *Nightclub, step 1.*

Figure 5-33   *Nightclub, step 2.*

Figure 5-34   *Nightclub, step 3.*

Figure 5-35   *Nightclub, step 4.*

Using Mixed Mediums to Render a Complex Environment

Overlooking a lobby

One of the quick ways to render a complex environment is to use a combination of marker, paint, watercolor, and colored pencil. The watercolor can give a basic tone and loose feeling to the drawing; the markers should render the structure of the space, in this case, a lobby; the colored pencils enhance the details; and paint may be overlapped and provide for a highlight.

Figure 5-36 shows that based on your material and color selection you should choose a group of watercolors or paints that you are going to use to create the basic tone and background of the drawing.

Because the water is absorbed into the paper, the surface probably will not stay flat, so you need to draw on heavier paper. One technique to keep the drawing surface flat is to glue the paper on a piece of cutable board such as plywood. To use this technique, turn your drawing over and put glue on the four edges. Then, turn it back over again and push hard on the edges to glue it to the board (see Figures 5-37 and 5-38). Be sure not to glue the drawing to your drafting board or table.

Use the wider flat brushes to mix several watercolors, which are based on your material selection, then apply a wash on your drawing surface. This process can quickly convey a basic tone to your drawing with unevenness and a feeling of motion. The tone should be a medium value of all your color selections (see Figure 5-39).

 TIP In general, a good background with a variety of colors can make it much easier to successfully integrate all objects that you are going to render. Do not mix the colors too much. Leave some strokes as texture.

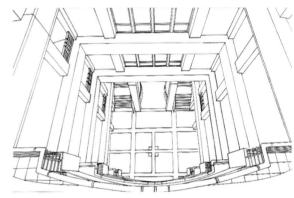

Figure 5-38 *A look into a lobby, step 3.*

Figure 5-36 *A look into a lobby, step 1. Decide on the tone of the space to select colors for the creation of the background.*

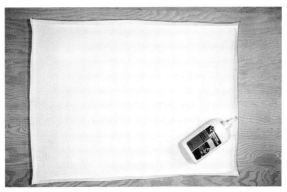

Figure 5-37 *The technique for keeping drawing surface flat.*

Figure 5-39 *A look into a lobby, step 4.*

Continually use watercolor to give the basic color to all the interior architectural elements, such as floor, beams, columns, walls, and railings. Also, in this step, define where the shadow and light are coming from (see Figure 5-40).

TIP By using watercolor and a brush you can define the shadow and light much quicker than using marker. The first two steps should be loose and quick.

The next stage is to do more refining. From this stage, you may start introducing markers to put in more details. Use several markers to draw the transition from light to dark. Refine more by using the fine tip of the marker and some colored pencils for the details. Also, in this step, refine your textures

and reflections more. The columns should be reflected onto the floor, and the floor should have a diagonal line to represent its shininess. The shadows from the window should be stronger close to the window, then they should fade out (see Figure 5-41).

The last stage is to reorganize and to give some unity to the drawing. Make sure you are concentrating on the elements closest to you. For example, the first railing or the first supporting column should have more detail than others farther away. Maybe the floor is too strong or the highlight is too strong, so use light- or medium-color markers to reduce the strong contrast. Focus lots of detail on the first columns and the first two layers of the railing. Distance and textures are essential to add at this stage (see Figure 5-42).

Figure 5-40 *A look into a lobby, step 5.*

Figure 5-41 *A look into a lobby, step 6.*

Figure 5-42 *A look into a lobby, step 7.*

Looking into a lobby

Follow the same procedure as previously
described to finish this exercise (see Figures
5-43 through 5-46).

Figure 5-43   *Lobby entrance, step 1.*

Figure 5-44   *Lobby entrance, step 2.*

Figure 5-45   *Lobby entrance, step 3.*

Figure 5-46 *Lobby entrance, step 4.*

Rendering of Building Exteriors

Computer-generated wire frame with manual rendering

More and more we are using the computer to help us generate perspective drawings so we can have enough optional views to visualize our design. The challenge is how to maximize the strengths of each medium. When we render a computer-generated frame, we need to think beyond just conventional techniques for manual rendering but consider how the rendering process can balance the two mediums. A computer-generated wire frame seems to have less of a human feel, but provides accuracy for our perspective. Manual rendering can provide the human touch to balance the machine drawing. You may relate the rendering process mentally to an hourglass in the following ways: (1) Begin with understanding the feeling of the design to be rendered; (2) apply related design elements; and (3) focus on detail and add the personal touch that defines the design's character.

Step 1: You can bring human emotion to computer-generated lines by using wide brushes and strokes in a variety of colors that represent the atmosphere of the drawing. The emotion should show in the brush strokes, with broad swipes of the arm and a twist of the torso (see Figure 5-47).

Step 2: Focus on all the design elements, such as lighting, materials, and surfaces. The emotion is a little more restricted, but the personal expression should still show through the different brush strokes. Pay particular attention to the subtle relationships between materials and lighting. The emotion should be balanced with the technical aspect of the design (see Figure 5-48).

Step 3: Concentrate on the technique and the refinement of materials to achieve details (see Figure 5-49).

Step 4: Set aside all limitations and put emotions in the drawing artistically (see Figures 5-50 and 5-51). You may use Figures 5-52 to 5-54 as reference when rendering similar spaces and buildings.

TIP Steps 1 and 2 can be done using watercolor brushes. Steps 3 and 4 should be done using colored pencil and marker for refining details. Gouache provides some highlight.

Figure 5-47 *Office tower, step 1.*

Figure 5-48 *Office tower, step 2.*

Figure 5-49 *Office tower, step 3.*

Figure 5-50 *Office tower, step 4.*

Figure 5-51 *Office tower, step 5.*

Figure 5-52 *Lobby.*

Figure 5-53 *Great Wall museum.*

Figure 5-54   *The Ninth and Franklin Streets Office Tower, designed by Marcellus Wright Cox & Smith, Architects, Richmond, Virginia.*

Appendix

Outline Drawings for Exercises

The outline drawings included in this appendix are for you to practice the rendering techniques explained in the preceding chapters. You may make copies first and render on the copies. When you practice, you may follow the step-by-step process described in the book.

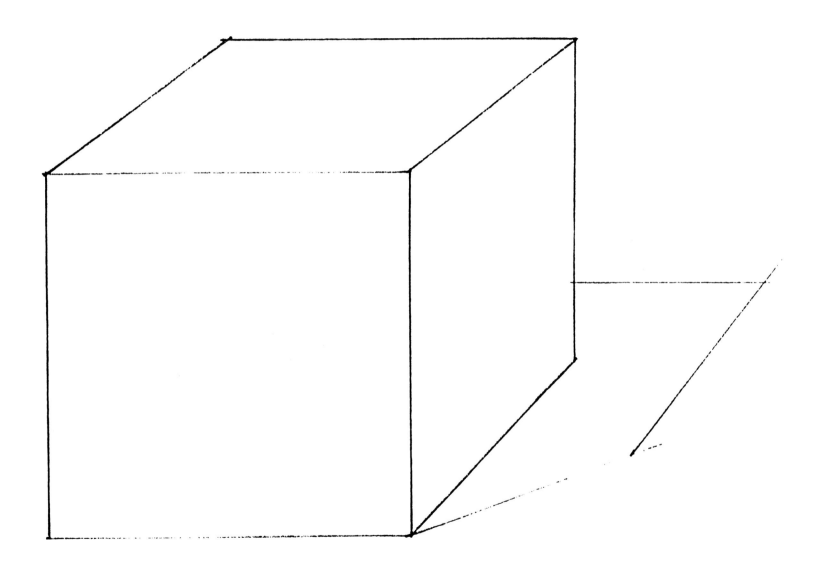

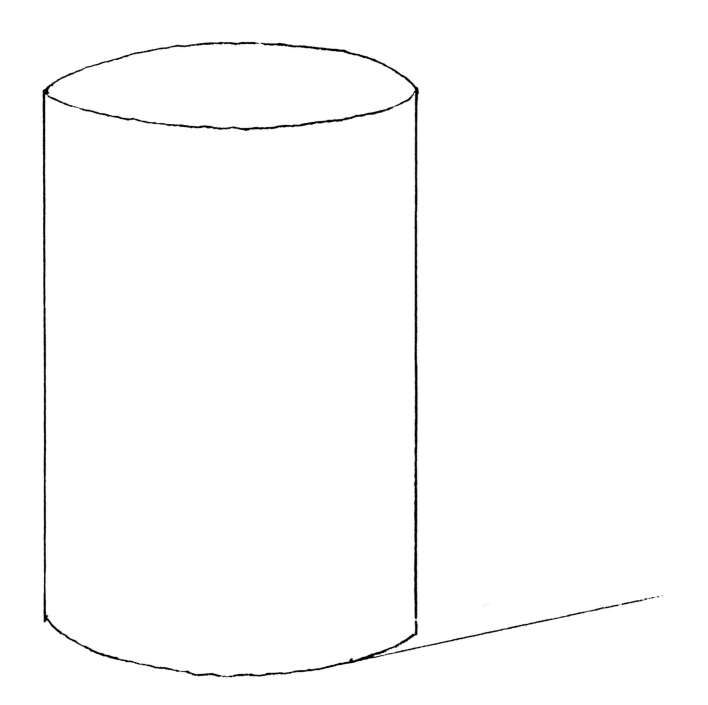

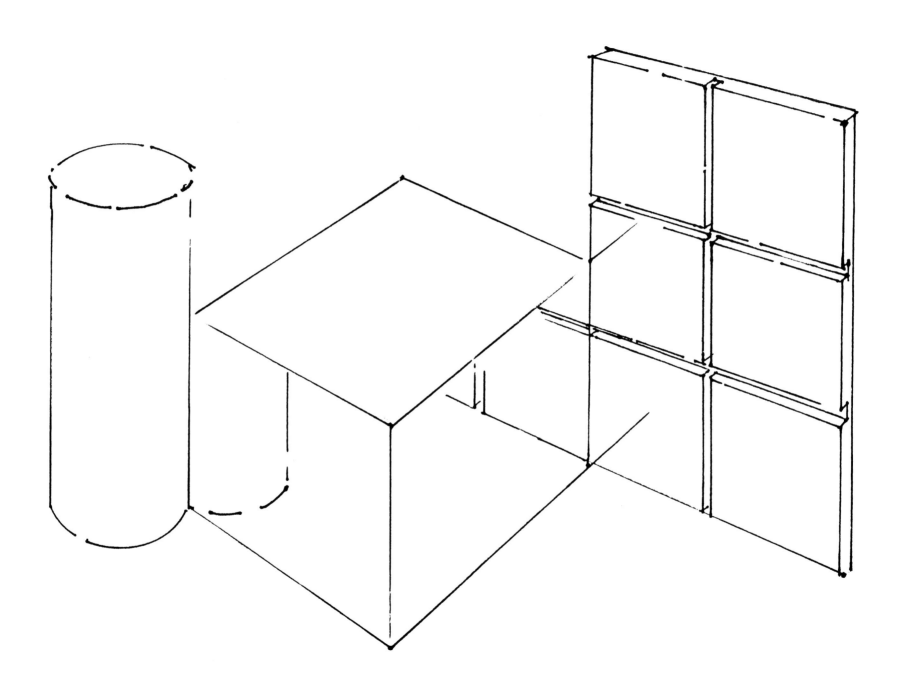

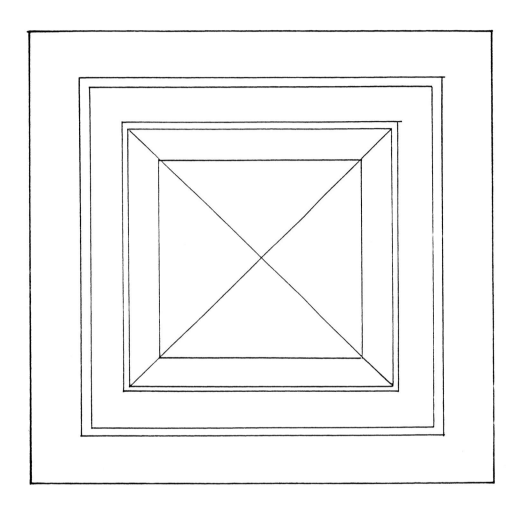

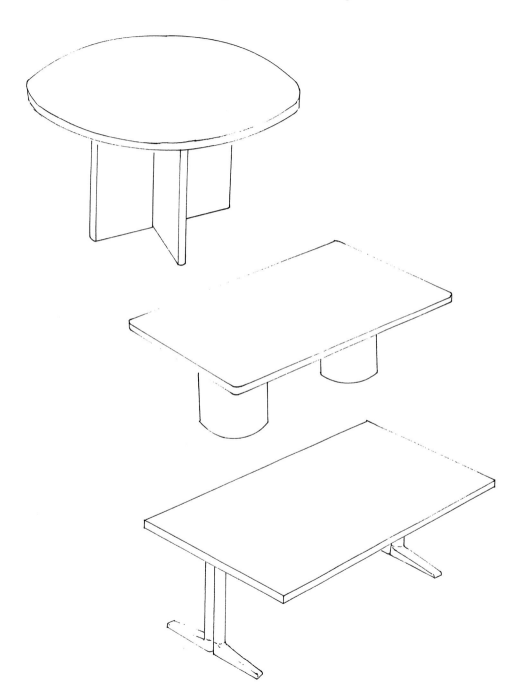

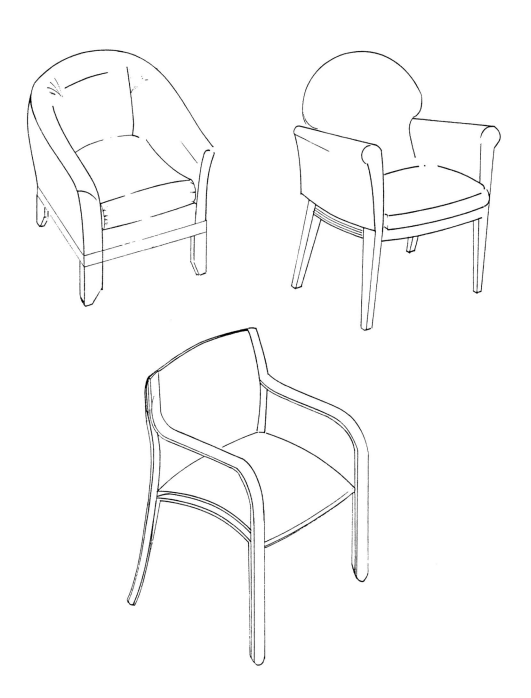

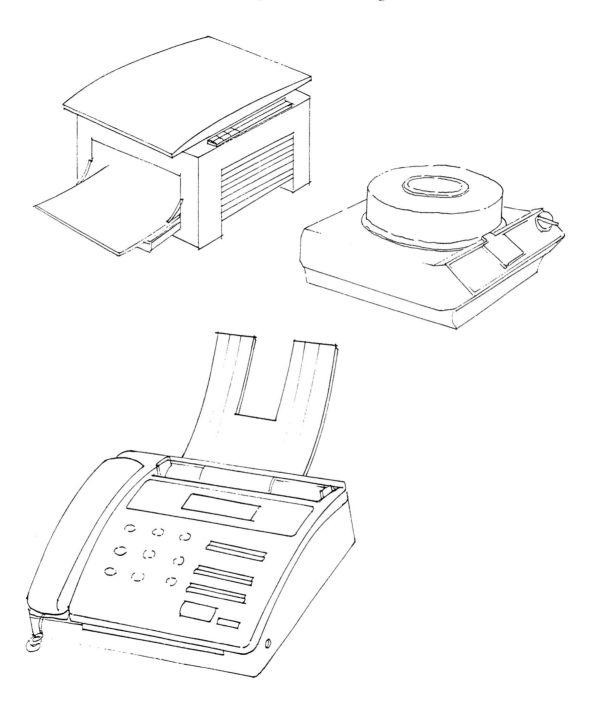

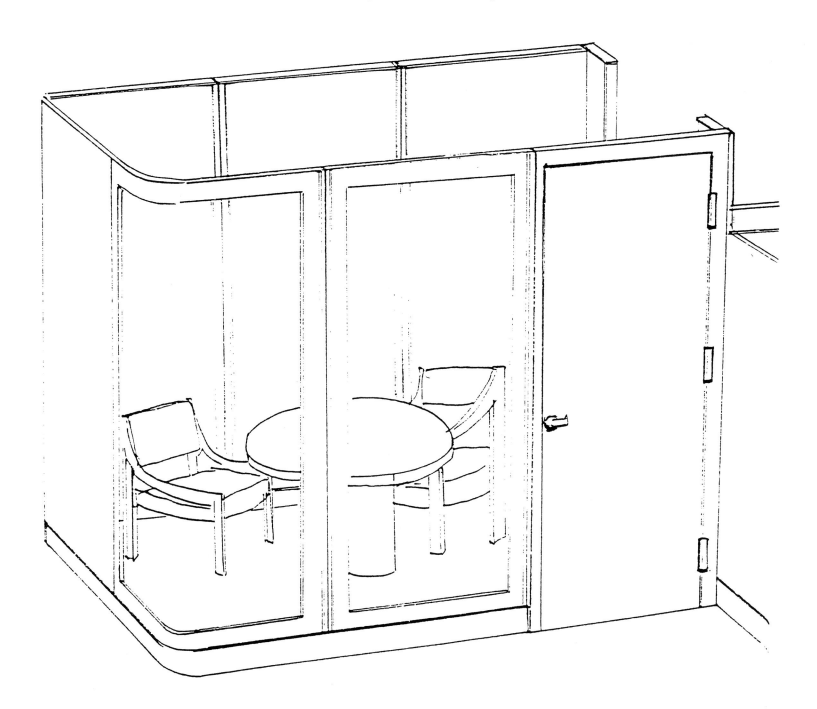

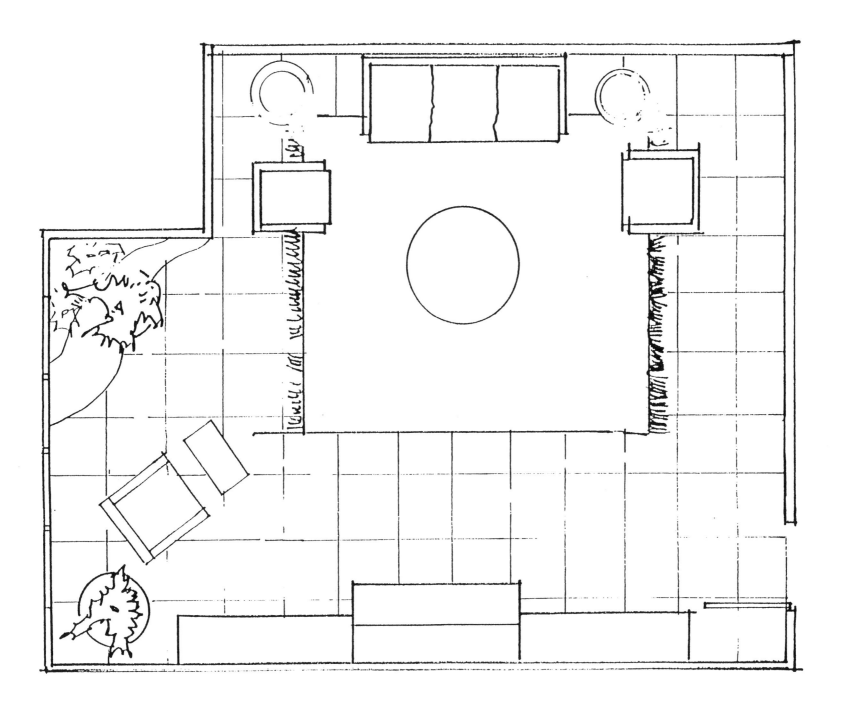

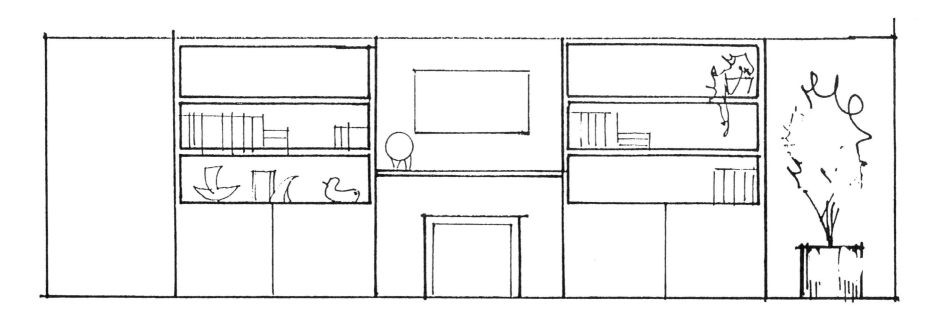

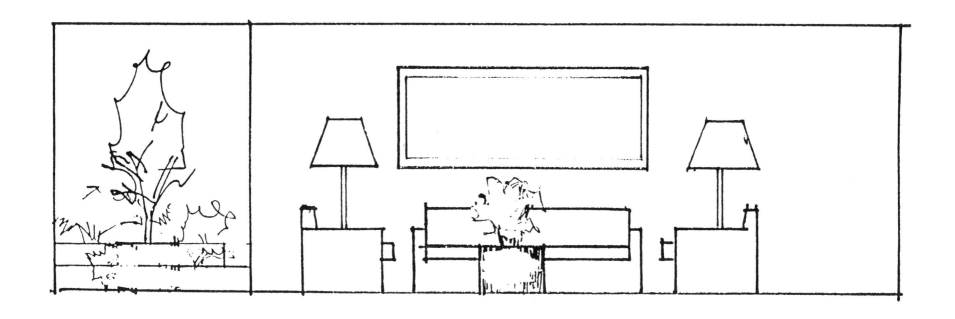

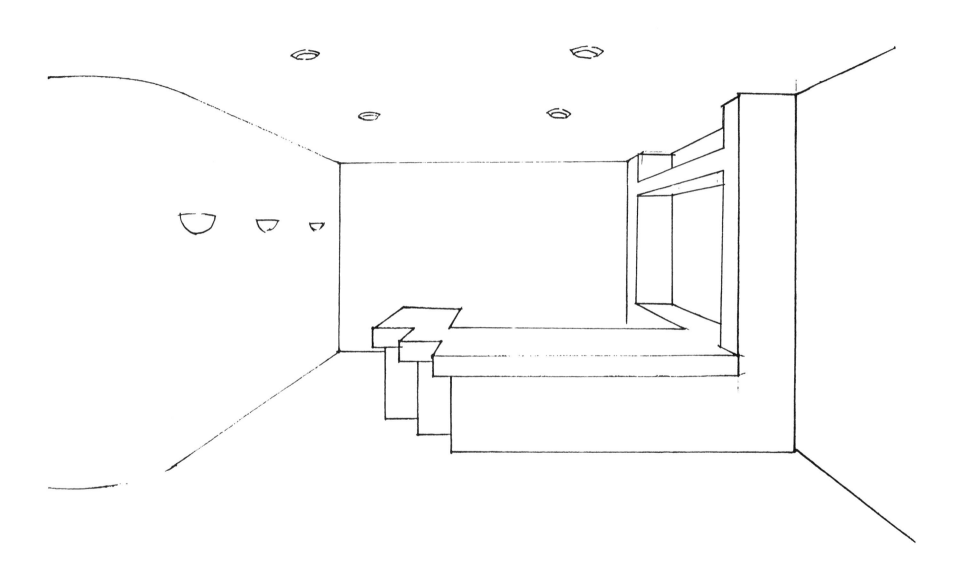

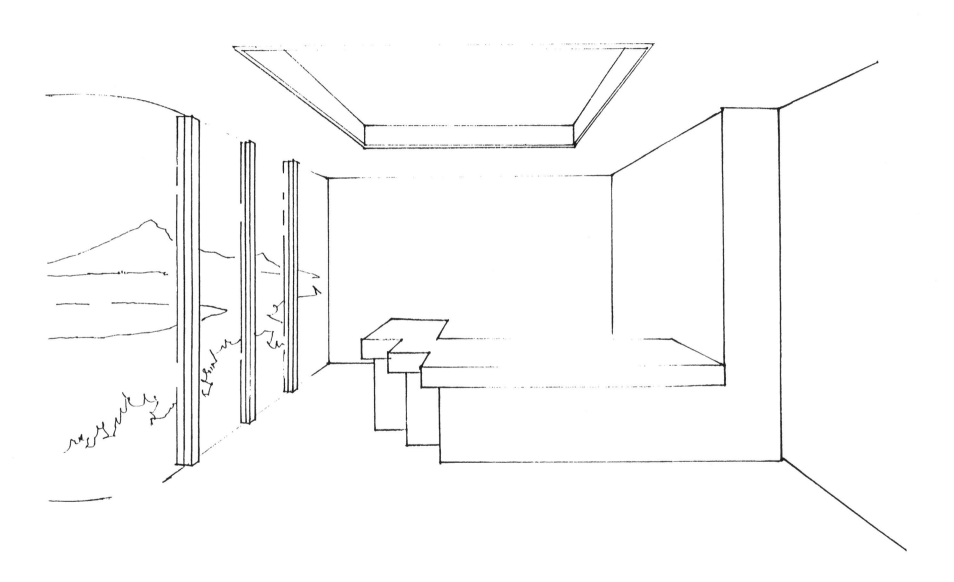

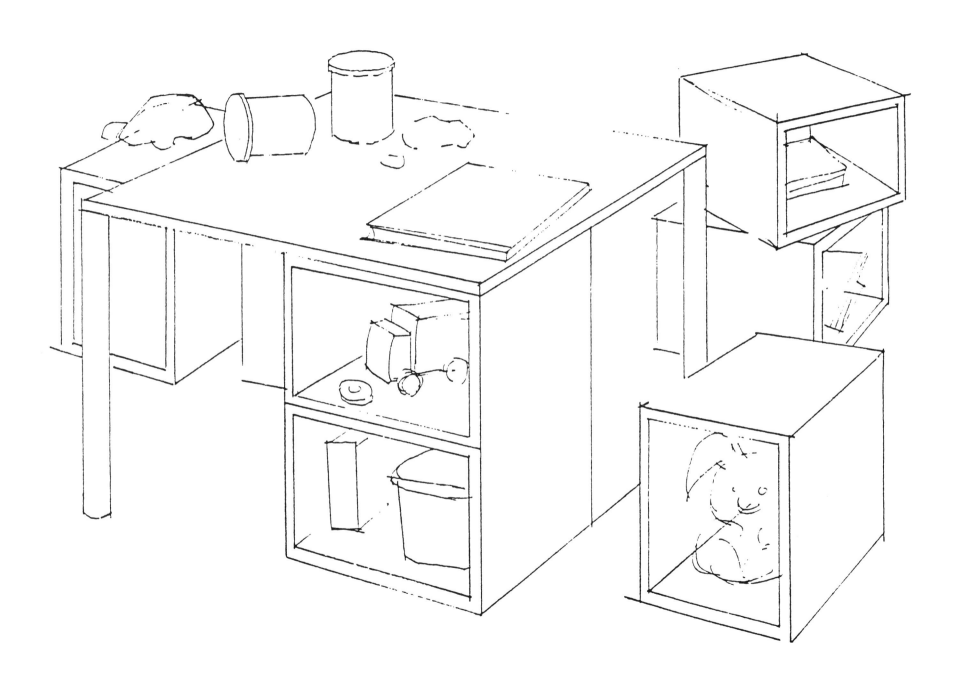

Bibliography

There are books on the market that cover a variety of rendering techniques and mediums. This bibliography lists some of these valuable sources.

Borgeson, Bet. *The Colored Pencil: Key Concepts for Handling the Medium.* New York: Watson-Gutpil Publications, 1993.

———. *Colored Pencil Fast Techniques: Methods and Strategies for Gaining Speed and Improving Your Work.* New York: Watson-Gutpil Publications, 1988.

Chen, John. *Architecture in Pen and Ink.* New York: McGraw-Hill, 1994.

Doyle, Michael E. *Color Drawing: A Marker/Colored-Pencil Approach for Architects, Landscape Architects, Interior and Graphic Designers, and Artists.* New York: Van Nostrand Reinhold Company, 1981.

Koplar, Richard. *Architectural Studies: A Step-by-Step Guide to Rendering and Drawing Techniques.* New York: McGraw-Hill, 1993.

Lockard, William Kirby. *Design Drawing Experiences.* Tucson, Arizona: Crisp Publications, 1977.

Sakaizumi, Ryo. *Marker Drawing: Practical Presentation Technique.* Tokyo, Japan: Graphic-sha Publishing Company, 1991.

Index

Page numers in italics refer to figures.

About the Author

Wei Dong is a professor of interior design at the University of Wisconsin-Madison. He formerly taught at Iowa State University and the Beijing Institute of Architecture and Design. A graduate of Virginia Commonwealth University (M.F.A. in Interior Environment) and Beijing's Central Academy of Arts and Design (B.A. in Interior Design), he has worked professionally at Marcellus Wright Cox & Smith and other firms. The recipient of numerous awards for excellence in teaching, and a frequent participant in national and international design exhibits, Wei Dong also gives presentations and workshops on design visualization and rendering at universities and firms.